KANGCHENJUNGA
A Trekker's Guide

The trail down to Dobhan rewards with stunning views almost every step of the way

KANGCHENJUNGA
A Trekker's Guide

by
Kev Reynolds

CICERONE PRESS
MILNTHORPE, CUMBRIA, UK

ISBN 1 85284 280 6
A catalogue record for this book is available from the British Library.
Photographs © K. Reynolds

DEDICATION

This book is for Roger Shinn - who should have been with us.

ACKNOWLEDGEMENTS

Once again I am grateful to Cicerone Press for their continued support
and encouragement, and for providing me with so many excuses to
spend happy months roaming the world's finest mountain ranges.
Frank McCready, of Sherpa Expeditions in London, gave me my first
opportunity to visit Kangchenjunga in 1989, and I shall always be
thankful to him for that - and to the enthusiasm of Bart Jordans who led
that trek. Since then my good friend Kirken Sherpa, who runs Himalayan
Paradise Trekking & Mountaineering in Kathmandu, has taken care of
the logistics for many of my travels in the mountains of Nepal, and it is
he and his first-rate crew to whom I owe sincere thanks for organising
the trek to both north and south base camps of Kangchenjunga that
formed the basis of research for this guidebook. Sharing those trails
were: Alan Payne, Wendy Parkin, Caroline Grazebrook, Julia Mockett,
Keith and Kathy Howard, and my wife, Linda (Min), while Mila and
Bimbadhur ('Beam') are singled out for special thanks since their care
and consideration were second to none. Their quiet smiles reflect the
generous friendship to be found among the people of Nepal, while
Kirken is the epitome of Sherpa dependability. My sincere thanks to
them all.

Kev Reynolds

Cicerone guides by the same author:

Annapurna - a Trekker's Guide
Everest - a Trekker's Guide
Langtang, Gosainkund & Helambu - a Trekker's Guide
Walking in the Alps
Walks in the Engadine - Switzerland
The Valais
The Bernese Alps
Ticino - Switzerland
Central Switzerland

The Jura (with R.B. Evans)
Alpine Pass Route
Chamonix to Zermatt - the Walker's Haute Route
Tour of the Vanoise
Walks & Climbs in the Pyrenees
Walking in Kent Vols I & II
The Wealdway & The Vanguard Way
The South Downs Way & The Downs Link
The Cotswold Way

Front cover: Chang Himal (Wedge Peak) soars above the left bank of the Kangchenjunga Glacier

CONTENTS

PREFACE

After he had climbed Kangchenjunga from the north-west with Doug Scott and Joe Tasker in 1979, the late Peter Boardman commented to a friend that the walk to the base of the mountain had been the most beautiful he had ever undertaken. Coming from a man who had climbed in many visually spectacular ranges around the world, that says much. With the opening of the far north-east of Nepal to trekkers in 1988, others too have since discovered that the trek to Kangchenjunga is a strong contender for the title of 'The Most Beautiful Walk in the World'.

This book is a guide to that trek. It describes the trails, villages and views, gives a potted history of some of the mountains, and seeks to add background interest for anyone planning to visit Kangchenjunga for themselves. But what it cannot do by words alone is unfold the full grandeur of this amazing region. It cannot adequately express the daily wonder of being drawn into scenes of exquisite beauty, nor reveal the delight that comes from mixing (albeit briefly) with people of a different race, a different cultural background, with a different set of values. It is quite possible that it is these you will cherish most, and remember long after your return - for the wonder of these things will come from within, will be a response to the way you react to a wealth of experiences on offer. Trekking among the world's highest mountains may be to some little more than a physically active holiday amidst wild and dramatic scenery. That may be all that one will ask, but it can be (should be?) something more than that. It is up to each one of us to make of it what we will.

Although there are fewer opportunities for cultural interaction on this trek than may be had in most other parts of trekkers' Nepal, due to the fact that it is a sparsely populated region, the Rai, Limbu and Bhotiya settlements that do exist along the trail will certainly add something of value to your travels - if you allow them. How successfully you interact with the villagers, and with your trekking crew, will depend upon your sensitivity, and the degree to which you intend to make the most of the privilege of being there.

First of all forget any notion of superiority, any idea that the ways of the West are better than those of Nepal and its economically impoverished population. For here you will find a society that has developed at a more sedate pace and in a different direction to ours; it

7

has priorities that we may find difficult to understand, values that we simply do not own. But if you care to look, you will find that there are riches here of a kind long lost to our own materialistic society. Instead of dismissing them, listen, observe, and on occasion use your senses in place of refined Western intellect. If you can grow receptive to the ways of others, you will come away enriched.

Since Kangchenjunga lies in a very remote corner of the country, and the trekking routes described in these pages are among the toughest yet open to commercial groups in Nepal, it is likely that most who attempt them will already have experience of trekking elsewhere in the Himalaya. But it is also possible that there will be some for whom this will be their very first visit, their first experience of such a demanding, multi-day journey. They, perhaps, may need to understand that trekking among big mountains leads occasionally into potentially dangerous situations. It is no use pretending otherwise, nor ignoring the fact that every year accidents happen. Trekkers are injured by falling rocks, or by the horns of passing yaks; some die of hypothermia, or of acute mountain sickness. Some simply fall from the trail due to a momentary loss of concentration. So all who wander there should remain alert, be vigilant to the possibility of landslip, stonefall, crumbling paths and greasy rocks, and remember that Nepal has no organised mountain rescue service such as we have in Britain and the European Alps. Should an accident occur self-help may well be the only option.

All who follow routes described in this book should assume responsibility for their own safety, and look to the needs of those with them. This includes porters and all members of the trek crew, as well as their fellow trekkers.

Trail information outlined in the following pages reflects as accurately as possible those routes experienced during research. Nonetheless, the Himalaya is by no means a static range and even without human intervention foothills, middle hills and the big mountains alike are in a constant state of flux, with regular changes to the landscape being made by courtesy of avalanche, landslide, rockfall and the annual monsoon, which is here greater than almost anywhere in the Himalaya. Note that paths may be re-routed and bridges replaced, thanks to such influences, while the size of villages, and the number of teahouses and camping areas, are bound to increase as Kangchenjunga's appeal to trekking and mountaineering expeditions becomes better known. Any such changes that affect the trek in any meaningful way will be noted in future editions of this guide, and I'd appreciate the help of trekkers in keeping me updated. A postcard addressed to me via the publisher will be received with gratitude.

Please be aware that heights quoted may not be entirely accurate. Although readings were taken at frequent intervals along the trail, having few opportunities to calibrate the altimeter with generally accepted altitudes, discrepancies are inevitable over a period of several weeks on trek. Distances given should also be taken as a rough guide only, for although several maps were consulted when attempting to measure the length of each day's journey, I draw the conclusion that not one truly represents the country as it is in reality. I look upon that as a bonus, and invite readers to do likewise.

As for times given for each stage, these indicate how long it took to walk from village to village, or from camp to camp, and represent the pace of a reasonably fit group of trekkers. These figures are based on actual walking times and make no allowances for rest stops, photographic delays or lunch breaks. On some days such stops can virtually double the time quoted. But each trekker, or group of trekkers, will have their own speed; some will therefore be faster, others slower, than mine. Use the times quoted as intended - as a rough indication of the length of each stage, not as a challenge. And perhaps you too will later respond as I do, when asked again and again how far you walked, that actual distance has little meaning; what is important is how many hours of enjoyment you can squeeze from each day.

On this trek it should be twenty-four.

Kev Reynolds
Kent, spring 1998

At the time of publication permits are
only officially issued to those trekking in
a group organised by a recognised agent.

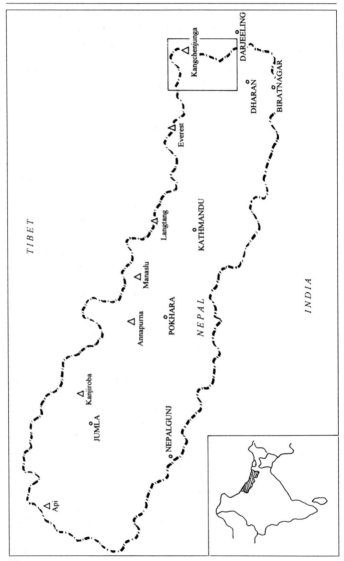

INTRODUCTION

*"It is always interesting to roam with ... a mountain people,
through their thinly inhabited valleys, over their grand mountains,
and to dwell with them in their gloomy and forbidding forests, and
no thinking man can do so without learning much, however
slender the means at his command for communion."*

(Sir Joseph Dalton Hooker: *Himalayan Journals*)

Joseph Hooker was not only one of the greatest of British botanists,
he was also a man who loved to travel in wild and unknown
country, and in 1848-49 he made two pioneering journeys in the
Himalaya during which he almost reached the base of
Kangchenjunga - the first through Nepal, the second in Sikkim - and
the account of his travels recorded in the two volumes of his classic
Journals makes fascinating reading one hundred and fifty years on.

Whilst the Western world would hardly be recognised by
Hooker and his contemporaries today, Kangchenjunga, its valleys
and villages, seem hardly to have changed at all, and the comments
quoted above with regard to learning much from roaming with "a
mountain people through their thinly inhabited valleys [and] over
their grand mountains" remains as true now as when it was first
written. Following trails described in this present guidebook
provides the modern-day trekker with ample opportunities to do
just that.

Straddling the border with Sikkim in the far north-eastern
corner of Nepal, Kangchenjunga (8586m: 28,169ft) is the world's
third highest mountain, a huge massif with five main tops and five
great glaciers dominating a spur that projects southward from the
main Himalayan axis, likened by F.S. Smythe to "a rugged peninsula
[jutting] from the main Himalayan coast". Long considered sacred,
its Tibetan name (Kang-chen-dzö-nga) has been translated as 'The
Five Treasures of the Great Snows'. Although some claim this to be
a reference to its five distinct summits, it is more likely to stem from
the number of glaciers flowing from it.

It is a fabulous massif with several outstanding satellite peaks of striking individuality whose characteristic outlines signal from afar. Jannu, or Kumbhakarna to give its Nepalese name, is the most obvious of these, but there are others. In fact the head of several parallel valley systems are simply bursting with drama and magnetic appeal.

Until Nepal opened its borders rather tentatively in 1949, Kangchenjunga and its immediate neighbours were probably the best-known mountains in the entire Himalayan chain, thanks to the clear view obtained of them from Darjeeling, that great hill station of the British Raj, some 70 kilometres away, and the fact that access to the south-eastern side had been established for a hundred years and more. Moreover, several expeditions had made attempts to climb it from both sides of the border, but always starting from Sikkim, and as early as 1899 D.W. Freshfield had made an almost complete circuit of the massif.

However, once Nepal relaxed its borders, Sikkim became off-limits to travellers from the West, and Kangchenjunga slipped into a shadowy semi-oblivion as other Himalayan mountains (Everest and Annapurna are obvious examples) became the focus of attention for mountaineers and, more especially in the context of this guide, for a growing number of trekkers. Although Kangchenjunga was climbed just two years after Everest, the approach via the Nepalese foothills remained out of bounds to all but a few select expeditions until 1988. Only then was the full majesty of the far north-east of Nepal revealed to an eager vanguard of adventurous travellers. Since then Kangchenjunga has taken its rightful place in the trekking world as the connoisseur's mountain.

But apart from the obvious attraction of its mountains, the whole region is considered so special that at the time of writing plans are in progress by the World Wildlife Fund and the National Parks and Wildlife Protection Department of the Nepalese Government to dedicate the border regions (Nepal, Tibet and Sikkim) as a 'protected park' by the year 2000. This is in recognition of several endangered wildlife species found here: snow leopard, musk deer, red panda, grey wolf and Himalayan black bear.

TREKKING KANGCHENJUNGA

"The track led us through wonderful scenery, at times along the crest of the ridge, at others between rice-terraces, across open slopes, past tangles of rhododendrons and small villages."

(Franz Lindner: *The Mountain World 1964-65*)

Trekking to Kangchenjunga provides a very different kind of experience to that of more mainstream routes in Nepal. It is a thinly populated region with a greater sense of isolation than will be felt in more easily-accessible areas such as Langtang, Annapurna and even Khumbu (Everest), and just to get to the start of the trek involves either a two-day bus journey from Kathmandu, flight to a remote airstrip, or a combination of air and road via Biratnagar in the Terai. Trails too are rougher, facilities for trekkers more primitive, routes less well defined. Since there are few opportunities to buy provisions along the way, all foodstuffs need to be carried in. This means porters. And porters to carry food for the porters.

At the time of writing permits are only officially issued to those trekking in a group organised by a recognised agent. However, I know of a few intrepid individuals who have managed to sweet-talk their way to obtaining permits to trek to Kangchenjunga without an agency set-up, but they have found it a tough proposition, having to backpack huge loads and take what lodging they could along the way. Teahouses and lodges are at present being developed, but as yet these are extremely basic, even by standards set in other regions of the Himalaya, although these are likely to improve as the demand grows. At present so-called 'hotels' are often of more value in housing porters than all but the most impecunious of Western trekkers.

✳   ✳   ✳

There are three possible approach routes and two main destinations to the Kangchenjunga trek. Two foothill routes, one beginning at the present roadhead of Basantpur, the other at the STOL (Short Take-Off and Landing) airstrip at Tumlingtar, converge at Dobhan on the west bank of the Tamur Khola after crossing the scenic Milke Danda crest. Both of these approaches reward with cultural interest and

13

fabulous views to Makalu, Lhotse and Mount Everest to the north-west, and to Jannu, Kangchenjunga and the Singalila Ridge to the north-east. The third approach begins at the STOL airstrip at Suketar above the township of Taplejung to the east of Dobhan, and is used by groups requiring a shorter trek than demanded by the other two.

Both the main destinations enjoy spectacular locations on the edge of glaciers and with huge mountain walls soaring above. Pangpema, commonly known as Kangchenjunga North Base Camp, is at 5140 metres (16,864ft), while Oktang (4780m: 15,682ft) is an amazing viewpoint from a *chorten* set on a moraine on the south side of the mountain.

Between these two runs a high ridge of mountains which separates the valleys of the Ghunsa and Simbua Kholas, and for well-acclimatized trekkers with sufficient time at their disposal, there are two possible routes across this ridge linking the route to Pangpema with that of Oktang. The higher and more difficult of these crossings is via the 5258 metre (17,251ft) Lapsang La, the second and more popular is by way of three linking passes which are, naming from west to east, Sinion La (4660m: 15,289ft), Mirgin La (4675m: 15,338ft) and an unnamed pass at about 4720 metres (15,486ft). (Note that there is confusion over which *La* is which on this second crossing. Some authorities say that the Mirgin La comes before the Sinion La, others name the Sinion La first. On my last crossing a local man from Ghunsa came with us, and he stated that the first pass is the Sinion La. Not that any of this matters, of course.)

The following brief outlines provide an overview of possibilities, more precise details of which are provided in the main body of text later in the book.

The Foothills:

Basantpur to Dobhan: (3-4 days)

From the roadhead at Basantpur well-used trails snake up to and across the rhododendron-clad ridge of the Tinjure Danda, and over broad pastures with big views, through such villages as Chauki, Manglebari and Gupha Pokhari to the crest of the Milke Danda. This too is lush with rhododendrons and from it more wide vistas are enjoyed before making the long descent to Dobhan at the confluence of the Maiwa Khola and Tamur River.

Tumlingtar to Dobhan: (4 days)

From the airstrip at Tumlingtar the way crosses the Hinwan Khola and begins a long climb to the neatly paved brass-makers' village of Chainpur, from which sunset views on Makalu are very fine. At Chainpur there is a choice of trails. One heads east to Chauki, the other goes north-east to the scattered village of Nundhaki where there is another choice of routes. One cuts round the flank of the Milke Danda to Gupha Pokhari where it joins the Basantpur-Dobhan trail, while the other climbs steeply to cross the Milke Danda, then descends through terraced farmland to Dobhan.

To Kangchenjunga North Base Camp:

Dobhan to Pangpema: (9-10 days)

It takes about three days to trek north-east along the valley of the Tamur River, keeping to the east bank all the way, before coming to Sokathum at the confluence of the Tamur and Ghunsa Khola. This is an undulating route, while the initial stage up the narrow, gorge-like valley of the Ghunsa Khola is a remorselessly steep climb to Amjilassa. Thereafter the way eases a little, but it's still demanding enough to Gyapra, Phole and Ghunsa. Beyond Ghunsa there are landslides to cross and huge mountains dominate all views at Khambachen. Assuming everyone is acclimatized here it will take a further two days to reach Pangpema overlooking the Northwest Face of Kangchenjunga.

To Kangchenjunga South:

Taplejung to Ramze & Oktang: (8-9 days in - 6-7 days out)

The shortest trek to Kangchenjunga leads to the Simbua Khola (Yalung Glacier) side of the mountain from Taplejung airstrip (flights from Biratnagar and/or Kathmandu) and takes from eight to nine days. Allow an extra day if you join this route from one of the above approaches to Dobhan. This is quite a tough route with much height gain and loss, through forests and cultivated hillsides, with many villages until you reach Yamphudin after about four days. Thereafter the country is very sparsely populated. Once you gain the valley of the Simbua Khola there are just a few yak pastures and (in 1997) very basic teahouses. The viewpoint of Oktang is usually visited from a camp at Ramze.

Pangpema to Ramze & Oktang: (5-6 days)
Whether you plan to cross the intervening ridge to the Simbua Khola by the Sinion La-Mirgin La route or via the Lapsang La, two days should be allowed to return from Pangpema to Ghunsa. Another two days will be needed to cross to Tseram from which fit trekkers could walk to Oktang and back in a longish day. The better option would be to make another camp at Ramze and spend more time up at Oktang before heading down again.

* * *

For those of us who have trekked there the stark beauty and undisputed grandeur of the region has become the very stuff of dreams. Wandering along foothill ridges in the first few days of the trek is to sample all the vivid contrasts for which Nepal is justly famous: the gentle warmth, the terraced hills and thatched houses, flowers and fruit, seething insects and birds - and ahead, the enthralling vision of the vertical arctic world of the Himalaya whose mountains hang suspended above the clouds.

Then come the middle hills with deep and narrow valleys, steep hillsides and a distinct change of vegetation with forests reminiscent of the European Alps and gentians blooming beside the trail. No more Rai or Limbu villages, these hills are inhabited by Bhotiyas - people of Tibetan stock, whose prayer flags beat the winds, and water-driven prayer wheels capture the power of streams to scatter *Om Mani Padme Hum* to the four corners of the earth.

Each of these preliminary zones is special. But once you enter that upper world of almost barren valleys, so you become drawn through an avenue of awesome peaks 6000, 7000 and 8000 metres high. Tumultuous glaciers carve their silent trenches while snow-fluted peaks scrape the sky. Wherever you gaze there are scenes of grandeur that defy description but etch themselves as icons on the mind. For all its distant magnetism, Kangchenjunga itself becomes one of the least of these, surrounded as it is by so many amazing peaks.

For scenic wonders, the trek to Kangchenjunga is in a class of its own.

ON TREK

"There will, doubtless, always be mountain-lovers and mountaineers, young as well as old, who are something more than invalids or athletes or mere tourists; who desire during their holidays to change their habits and mode of life as well as their climate."

(D.W. Freshfield: *Round Kangchenjunga*)

The above was penned long before trekking as we understand it became the answer to many an armchair nomad's dream. Yet Freshfield's attitude towards mountains was very much the same as those for whom this present book is written, for his travels during the late 19th and early 20th centuries took him striding across numerous exotic ranges, sometimes alone or with one or two like-minded friends, or with guides and a full complement of native porters. He, I feel sure, would have felt completely at home if he were able to return today to the Himalayan trails described in the following pages.

Trekking, as Hugh Swift once commented, brings an immediacy to life; life is instantaneous, "it's right before your eyes". But it does not suit everyone. If you have never trekked before, but have been seduced by the tales and photos of others, consider first if it is right for you. Play the following scenario, put yourself in the picture and see if the dream still holds. Imagine the cold grey light of dawn following a sleepless night. Imagine a raw wind blowing, snow flurries swirling round the tent or rain falling. Perhaps you are feeling a mite queasy from something you ate last night, or your whole body aches from exertions of the past few days. You have been told that the route ahead is a demanding one, with much height gain and loss before the next camp is set up. And the trek leader is cajoling you to put on your boots and start walking, when the very last thing you want to do is get out of your sleeping bag.

It can be just like that sometimes, when you find you are on a not-so-merry-go-round that will not stop until the trek is over. It is not all blue skies and sunshine, sweet smiles and views that stretch to the ends of the earth.

17

There will be times (I can virtually guarantee them) when it is difficult to have a decent wash for several days at a stretch, or nights when it's impossible to enjoy a restful sleep. Perhaps you find it difficult to acclimatize; maybe the diet is not to your liking or, if you are new to camping, you discover that you dislike sleeping in a tent - or resent sharing a communal latrine that is little more than a canvas sentry box over a hole in the ground. Perhaps the difficulty of maintaining strict standards of hygiene comes as an unwelcome surprise; there may be times of confusion, or of homesickness; times when your Western sensibilities are appalled by the different values accepted by those whose country you are wandering through.

Successful trekking demands an ability to adapt to a range of ever-changing circumstances - the need to set aside the habits of a lifetime and be a sponge to absorb a whole new world of experience.

Should you find that last prospect appeals, however; if you are inspired by such a challenge, if you are convinced that wandering among the most dramatic and awe-inspiring landscapes on earth, of mingling day by day with people of an entirely foreign culture, and that a sense of achievement at the end of the trek will out-balance the odd day of discomfort or misery - then trekking is for you. But should you have doubts, forget it. Don't waste your money and instead look for an alternative holiday. Four or five days into a three-week trek is not the time to realise you have made a mistake. Life is too short. The financial outlay required to undertake a three-week trek in Nepal should be sufficient spur to ensure you enjoy every moment of your time there. Don't waste it on doubts or inadequate preparation.

It may be that you are used to wandering the wilderness alone or with just a like-minded friend. If so you will soon discover that trekking the trails of Kangchenjunga is not a solitary experience, for the very reason stated above that only group treks are sanctioned at present. This means that you will most likely be accompanied by a crew of sherpas, cook, kitchen boys and porters. The larger the group, the more numerous the trek crew. If you have never trekked in this style before, preferring independence to sociability, you may be surprised at how enjoyable such travel can be. Having been privileged to trek the full variety of styles, ie: completely alone, with just one companion, with only Nepalis, as well as with groups of

Western trekkers, I have found much to commend each way. But when you are trekking with others (often strangers) in a group situation, you have to accept the fact that you may need to sacrifice personal choice on occasion in consideration of group preference, and be aware that a determined effort may be required to enjoy cultural interchange at villages en route, for when travelling with others it is all too easy to carry your own culture with you and become divorced from the very people who could add colour and richness to the experience.

※　※　※

A number of trekking agents in the UK and elsewhere organise treks to Kangchenjunga, and before you book your holiday you would be advised to shop around to see which trek best suits your requirements. Make a few phone calls, ask a few pertinent questions, and unless cost is absolutely imperative, do not automatically go for the cheapest on offer. Often you get what you pay for.

Assuming this is your first commercial trek, it may be helpful to introduce here the crew and its social structure, and provide an outline to the trekker's day.

The Western leader represents the trekking company with whom you have booked your holiday, and will be answerable to you throughout your stay in Nepal. It is he or she who assumes overall responsibility for the day-to-day running of the trek, but it is the Sirdar who in practice makes the most important decisions and who commands the crew. The Sirdar is employed by the local trekking agent who, in turn, is employed as a sub-contractor by the Western trekking company. It is the Sirdar who chooses the kitchen crew (the cook may well have his own kitchen boys) and a 'foreman' for the porters, and who hires and fires along the way as the need arises. In consultation with the Western leader he will choose campsites, where there is a choice, that is, and will orchestrate the rhythm of the trek to keep everyone happy.

Below Sirdar in the hierarchy comes the cook. This is usually a senior sherpa working his way through the ranks with the object of becoming a Sirdar in due course. He will have one or two (maybe more) kitchen boys as helpers, and it is this kitchen crew who put in the longest hours of anyone on trek, rising an hour or so before dawn and curling up at the end of a long day after everyone else has begun snoring.

Then come the sherpas who may, or may not, be ethnic Sherpas (Bhotiya people born in the Solu-Khumbu district near Mount Everest). Sherpas with a small 's' act as general dogs-bodies on trek. They will be the guides, tent-erecters and camp dismantlers, the 'carers' when someone falls sick or has difficulty keeping up with the rest of the group, the ever-cheerful trek personnel, the best of whom make their clients feel really special without being servile. If you treat them with respect, not as servants, and readily enjoy their friendship, the social interaction between trekker and crew can offer one of the most rewarding experiences of the whole trip. That goes for porters too, for the man or, in some cases, the woman who carries your baggage should not be considered merely as a human juggernaut, but as a professional whose labour enables you to have the holiday of a lifetime. Recognise this fact, and even if you haven't sufficient words of Nepali to ask about his home or family, a smile of gratitude and a greeting of *Namaste* will help create a bond. And at the end of the trek you will have an opportunity to show your appreciation in practical terms with a tip. (Tipping is expected by all the crew, and will be organised by the Western leader at the appropriate time.)

Many porters, incidentally, are subsistence farmers with a few fields of their own, who operate as porters during the trekking season in order to earn cash with which to buy essentials for their family. But on one trek recently one of my porters surprised me by admitting that he was an electronics engineer in Kathmandu! "I repair television sets," he told me, but had chosen to do some portering for a change in order to see a part of his country that otherwise he would never have an opportunity to visit.

The trekking day follows an established routine which partly mirrors life in the hills, in that it basically begins at sunrise and ends shortly after darkness falls. In a land with little or uncertain electricity there is no culture of after-dark entertainment, so all activity falls within the hours of daylight. The pattern of life on trek then is very much as follows:

6.00   The day begins with a mug of tea being brought to your tent.

6.15   A bowl of warm washing water arrives at the tent door.

6.30   Pack kitbag ready for porters to make up their loads. Ensure you have all you'll need during the day in a small rucksack.

7.00   Breakfast. This often consists of porridge or cereal, eggs and chapatis, tea, coffee or hot chocolate. Unless the weather is really bad, you'll no doubt eat this outdoors as tents are collapsed and packed.

7.30   Start trekking. At this time of day the light is often pure, birds singing (in the foothills) and the air cool - great for photography. During the morning you'll overtake porters resting or cooking their first meal of the day; the kitchen crew should overtake, their loads rattling. If they don't overtake, you've gone too far and too fast and will probably have missed lunch!

11.00 Stop for lunch. The crew will usually have chosen a scenic spot, with water nearby. On arrival you'll be handed mugs of hot fruit drink. This is the time to rest, read, write notes, gaze at the scenery. Lunch is often a two-course meal, an example being tuna fish, fried potatoes, coleslaw and chapati, followed by tinned or fresh fruit and lots of tea.

13.00 Resume trekking, overtake porters resting by the trail, and in turn be overtaken by the kitchen crew and sherpas. Once again, if they don't overtake you, you've either taken a wrong trail or walked too fast and too far and missed camp. This is most unlikely as any good Sirdar will ensure a sherpa is ahead of you to mark the way at every trail junction.

16.00 Reach camp. Wash, wash clothes, relax with tea and biscuits, rejoice when the porter carrying your kitbag eventually arrives; air sleeping bag and make tent ready for the coming night. Place headtorch in an easy-to-locate position.

18.00 Dinner. Discuss the day and be given an outline of tomorrow's route by the Western leader. Dinner will invariably be a three-course meal, for example: soup; chicken, rice and vegetables; fresh fruit or maybe a pie or cake, followed by tea, coffee or hot chocolate.

20.00 To bed.

TREKKING SEASONS

"We used to await that magical moment when the rains cleared the haze in October."

(John Hunt: *The Alpine Journal, 1996*)

Lord (formerly Sir John) Hunt is perhaps best known as the leader of the first successful ascent of Mount Everest in 1953. But during his long service in the British Army out in India, he made several low-key but adventurous climbing expeditions to the Kangchenjunga range, especially during the 1930s, and in so doing became something of an authority on the mountains and their valleys. Accepting the fierce extremes of the monsoon in this part of the Himalaya, the comment quoted above may be appreciated in full, and echoed by those of us who are drawn year upon year to Nepal's seductive trails.

When choosing your trek to Kangchenjunga it is worth considering the most suitable season to go. In Nepal it is the monsoon and, of course, the harshness of winter, that dictate the trekking seasons. "All July," wrote W.W. Graham in a paper read before the Alpine Club in 1884, "and in Sikkim all August and September, the monsoon rages with a steady, perpetual south wind, bringing rain below and snow above." So trekking must be sandwiched between the end of the monsoon and the onset of winter, and the end of winter and onset of the next monsoon. If one were not to be put off by the heat, muddy trails, abundant leeches, daily rainstorms and limited views, it would be feasible to go trekking in the foothills throughout the summer months. Indeed, there are those who advocate it; the 'purists' (some might say masochists) who desire to have a very different experience to that of the more 'conventional' trekker for whom this guide is written. Most of us, though, are drawn by prospects of more settled conditions and crystal views.

Foothill trekking is also possible throughout the winter months, but severe cold and deep snow will effectively prevent the higher, more dramatic places and the high passes from being reached by all but the hardiest of mountaineers.

That leaves the pre-monsoon months of March, April and to

some extent, May, and post-monsoon season of October, November and the first half of December.

The pre-monsoon season rewards with spring flowers, and the abundant rhododendron forests should be truly memorable. The foothills can be very warm by day, especially during the latter part of the season, and in the build-up towards summer heat-haze will probably restrict views. However, the high country is usually clear, although occasional snowfall is not uncommon.

Post-monsoon is the classic time to trek in Nepal, with foothill and high mountain views throughout the latter half of October and November sparkling with clarity, the air having been effectively laundered by the long summer rains. In the high mountain valleys night-time temperatures may fall to -10°C or even -15°C while a bright sunny day can raise the thermometer to as much as 20°C. Foothill temperatures will be appreciably greater than these, of course. The weather is generally at its most settled during late-October and November, although a little light rain may be experienced on the foothill approach, and the odd day of snow at altitude is not unknown. On occasion a very heavy dump of snow may fall in the autumn, and it is the possibility of this that should make every prospective trekker go prepared for the worst, and also ensure that porters travelling with them are suitably attired. But on the whole autumn is a truly magical time in the Himalaya, and is by far the most popular season for trekking. As a consequence flights may be difficult to arrange except well in advance, and trails will be busier than at any other time of year.

PRE-TREK PREPARATIONS

"If you plan to trek...you should initiate or continue a good conditioning program."

(Hugh Swift: *Trekking in Pakistan and India*)

The late Hugh Swift knew all there was to know about trekking in the Himalaya - his two weighty but highly readable tomes, *Trekking in Pakistan and India* and *Trekking in Nepal, West Tibet and Bhutan*, are full of trail wisdom and anecdotal delights. When he advises the

23

need to be in good condition for trekking, one should take note.

"The art of Himalayan travel," said W.H. Murray, who also knew the big mountains from close confrontation, "is the art of being bold enough to enjoy life now." It is the ability to absorb as much of the landscape and its inhabitants as possible without detracting in any way from them. It comes from the use of all one's faculties and sensibilities; it is an enrichment that will heighten one's awareness. And the only way to ensure that every moment of the trek is enjoyed to the full, is to be both physically and mentally fit from day one. Do not be lulled into the belief that as porters will be carrying most of your gear you can slip easily into trekking mode and start to get fit on the walk-in. If that is your attitude, you will miss much of value in those initial stages - the very moments that set the stage for the weeks ahead. Trekking Kangchenjunga should add quality to your life. Make it a quality experience every step of the way.

In his excellent primer, *The Trekkers' Handbook*, Tom Gilchrist devotes several pages to ways of getting fit for trekking and makes the obvious point that "It is you who walks the trek - poor preparation equals poor performance, equals negative experience. In other words, your misery and discomfort preoccupy your thoughts, your holiday is ruined and you would be as well sitting on a bus as being out in Trekland."

There is probably no better way to get physically fit for trekking than to go walking - uphill and carrying a rucksack. In the weeks leading up to your holiday use stairs instead of lifts and escalators, and spend as many weekends taking long walks as you can, in hill or mountain country for preference to get your cardiovascular system (heart and lungs) well primed. Jogging and cycling for long distances are both useful means of building stamina and endurance, while swimming is beneficial since every muscle group is called into play and gently stretched.

The need for good *physical* fitness will be obvious to most prospective trekkers. In fact one of the most oft-asked questions is "How fit do I need to be?" What is less obvious is the need to be *mentally* fit. Yet this is every bit as important as - maybe even more important than - being physically in tune.

Consider for a moment: if you have never trekked a multi-day route through remote mountains before, you should ask yourself whether this particular trek is right for you. You may be physically able to cope with the rigours of the trail, of the constant gain and loss of altitude, the deep semi-tropical jungles and barren moraines, but unless you are mentally prepared to accept the very foreign-ness of the environment, as well as the need to walk on day after day for perhaps three weeks or so, with the knowledge that should anything go wrong you are a very long way from help, it may be better to look for a shorter, less demanding trek. If, however, these are all part of the appeal, read on.

Freshfield hit the nail on the head when he wrote of the need to change habit and mode of life as well as climate. Unless that need is addressed throughout the trek, you will not gain the full enjoyment such a journey so abundantly repays. A change of habit and mode of life implies the need to put Western values on hold and being prepared to accept that there could be much to learn about living from the hillfolk into whose land you step uninvited, and from the crew with whom you share each day. Learning to relax and to shrug aside the stresses that help make Western civilisation so uncivilised will close the gap between you and the people of Nepal. If you do that readily, look to each day with optimism and enthusiasm, and are determined to wring pleasure from each moment, you've a harvest waiting along the trail to Kangchenjunga.

PRE-TREK HEALTH

"Look to your health and if you have it, praise God, and value it next to a good conscience; for health is the second blessing that we mortals are capable of."

(Izaak Walton: *The Complete Angler*)

Physical fitness and a relaxed but positive attitude of mind offer unquestionable advantages when it comes to staying healthy on trek, but neither provide any immunity against disease. So, long before you go, make arrangements with your local GP or travel clinic to have those vaccinations recommended for trekking in

Nepal. (Try the *Yellow Pages* for details of your nearest Travel Clinic.) At the time of writing Nepal has no official vaccination requirements for entry unless, that is, your journey passes through a yellow fever infected area. However, it is advisable to protect yourself from a range of infectious diseases that can be prevented by either vaccine or prophylactic medicines.

Official health sources in the West currently advise the following immunisations: Typhoid, Tetanus, Meningococcal Meningitis, Polio and Hepatitis A. If you have had any of these immunisations previously, you may only need a booster. But check well in advance of travelling.

Hepatitis B is also on the list of possibilities. 'Hep. B' is transmitted through sex or by contact with contaminated blood, so you must assess for yourself the need for protection against this. Rabies could also be considered, although local research indicates that only one out of 6000 visitors is bitten by a suspect animal, so the risk is not high in the context of a month's travel in Nepal. Japanese Encephalitis has been added to the list in recent years, for this viral infection can be contracted when passing through rice paddies, and is especially prevalent during the monsoon, although local advice in Kathmandu suggests this is only necessary for anyone staying for more than a month in a suspect area - aid workers, for example. If in doubt check with MASTA (Medical Advisory Service for Travellers Abroad based at the London School of Hygiene and Tropical Medicine) who will send printed information sheets in response to a telephone request. The number to call is 0171 631 4408 (between 9.30am and 5.00pm Monday to Friday). Printouts are also available without charge at British Airways Travel Clinics for those attending for immunisation. In addition MASTA operates a Traveller's Health Line (01891 224100) which provides a health brief containing up-to-date information with regard to immunisations, the requirement for malaria prophylactic etc., and is tailored to specific regions. Note that the Department of Health also has a Helpline (0800 555 777) by which appropriate literature can be obtained free of charge.

As for malaria, this occurs throughout Nepal below 2000 metres, although Kathmandu and its valley are effectively malaria-free. The highest risk area is in the eastern Terai, through which the journey by road passes on the way to the Kangchenjunga region. It is therefore advisable to embark on a course of anti-malarial prophylactic. Those usually prescribed consist of two 250mg tablets per week of Chloroquine Phosphate (Avloclor is one brand name), plus two 100mg tablets daily of Proguanil Hydrochloride (Paludrin). The course begins one week before arrival in a suspect area, and continues for one month after leaving. In addition the following preventive measures should be taken to avoid being bitten by mosquitoes:

   1: Cover exposed skin after dusk.
   2: Use repellent spray.
   3: Sleep under an impregnated mosquito net.

Since dental care is non-existent in the region covered by this guidebook, it would be sensible to ensure you have no loose fillings or even the first sign of tooth decay before setting out on trek. Have a dental check-up at home, for there is nothing quite like high altitude, low temperatures and the nearest dentist being many days' walk away to set your teeth aching.

ON-TREK HEALTH

*"No one can appreciate good scenery when his digestion
is out of order."*

(Leslie Stephen: *The Playground of Europe*)

Reading too many articles or books relating to health problems in developing countries is likely to inspire one of two reactions. The first is to cancel your trek and stay cosseted at home, while the second leads to a rucksack bulging with the contents of your local pharmacy.

The following section has been compiled with the specific aim of breeding an awareness of problems that do exist, and of providing a clue as to how to deal with them. It is not intended to put anyone off. After all, the very exercise of trekking should be beneficial to health, increasing vitality and providing a warm sense of well-being. But if you listen to some trekkers, maintaining good health whilst away appears sometimes to be a major challenge. It needn't

27

be. Not only is it important to your overall enjoyment, it can be achieved with a little care and forethought. Just remain aware of potential problems, avoid complacency and use common-sense with regard to personal hygiene.

Water:
The first and major cause for concern is drinking water. Trekking is thirsty work. So is living at altitude where it is essential to drink copious amounts of liquid in order to stave off the effects of AMS (Advanced Mountain Sickness) - of which more later. But with poor sanitation throughout Nepal, no water should be considered safe to drink unless it has first been either boiled, filtered, treated with iodine, or comes in a bottle with an unbroken seal. That goes for the water supplied in Kathmandu hotels too, for a whole host of organisms surviving in the streams and rivers of Nepal can lay the unsuspecting low with a rich cocktail of ailments. Travelling with a reputable trekking company is probably as safe as you can get, however, for on group treks the kitchen crew is likely to be well aware of the need to boil all water for consumption, and you should have no cause for concern except, perhaps, in the highest camps where water may not boil at a high enough temperature to kill all bacterial spores. In this case an added precaution would be to treat your water with iodine tablets, if you can get them. If not, use 5-8 drops per litre of tincture of iodine, and allow to stand for 20 minutes before drinking - 30 minutes if the water is very cold. Note that iodine should not be taken if you are pregnant.

The same precautions should be applied in regard to water used for cleaning teeth. On a teahouse trek once I listened to a monologue given by a fellow trekker on the dangers of drinking untreated water, only to see him a couple of hours later rinsing his teeth under a standpipe. I wonder how long it took before he was suffering diarrhoea and blaming it on something he ate.

Personal Hygiene:
Maintaining a high standard of personal hygiene should be second nature, on and off trek, in order to prevent gastro-intestinal problems. That, however, is not quite so easy to live up to in the remote country of the high Himalaya where dusty trails and camping areas harbour

all sorts of nasties, and hot water for washing is a luxury. But you should try to be scrupulous with regard to keeping hands and fingers clean, not only as you sit down to eat, but throughout the day. A pack of baby wipes can be useful for this along the trail, while serious attention to soap and water in camp will lead to a feeling of smug cleanliness. For a while, at least.

Kathmandu Quickstep or Trekker's Trot:
Most trekkers suffer a mild dose of diarrhoea at some time during their stay in Nepal. Often this is just a short-lived reaction to a change of diet, or an after-effect of a long flight. But to be afflicted whilst on trek can be debilitating. "I felt dizzy and weak," said Mike Harding in *Footloose in the Himalaya*, "and dangerous at both ends."

As was suggested in the preceding section, such gastro-intestinal problems can be largely avoided by close attention to personal hygiene, and by not drinking untreated water. But food preparation is another major source of concern, and since prevention is better than cure, you should stay clear of salads and unpeeled fruit. These are temptations perhaps in Kathmandu, but are unlikely to be a problem on trek. Should you be served salads, though, check through your Western leader that it has first been soaked in iodine or potassium permanganate to kill any germs lurking in the lettuce. As for fruit, simply peel it or forget it. Again, the kitchen crew will have been trained to prepare all food with close attention to hygiene. The last thing a trek cook needs is for members of his group to go down with diarrhoea, for the finger of suspicion will immediately point his way.

But what if the bug does strike and Kathmandu Quickstep becomes the dance of the day? Take plenty of liquids to avoid dehydration, reduce solid food intake and avoid dairy products, coffee and alcohol. A bland diet of boiled rice, porridge, plain or salt biscuits should be sufficient to keep you on the move while the bug works its way through. A rehydration solution, such as Dioralyte or Jeevan Jal (the Nepalese brand available in Kathmandu), is rapidly absorbed into the system and will help replace lost body salts. If the problem persists after three or four days, break open the first aid kit and take Immodium. Only go for antibiotics as a last resort.

High on the list of likely suspects causing diarrhoea is a tiny one-celled organism called *Giardia lamblia* that survives not only in the glacial waters of Nepal, but also wherever nightsoil fertiliser (made largely from human faeces) is spread on the fields. When digested the parasite invades the upper part of the small intestine where it can damage the gut lining. After infection it may take two to three weeks (or much longer) before symptoms become apparent, and may then result in sudden acute illness - or have a more long-lasting effect. It is not life-threatening, although symptoms are distinctly anti-social. These include foul-smelling, rotten-egg gases being emitted, loose bowel movements, stomach cramps after eating, weight loss and dehydration. Fortunately treatment is straightforward with fairly rapid results. A course of tinizadole antibiotic (Tiniba - available from Kathmandu pharmacies) normally results in a complete cure: take 2gr in a single dose daily for three days. This should be taken one hour before food.

Throat and Chest Problems:

Coughs, colds and chest infections are exacerbated by sitting for long periods in smoky teahouses, by the dust of the trail and the dry cold air of high altitude. The sound of locals emptying their lungs with a serenade of coughing and spitting is the Himalayan dawn chorus to which most trekkers add voice at some time or other. Soluble lozenges will soothe inflamed throats, and catarrh pastilles are also worth taking. For sore, inflamed throats, try gargling a solution of two aspirin tablets dissolved in warm water - repeat at 6-hourly intervals.

Chest infections are usually marked by uncontrollable bouts of coughing, and the release of a lot of green-yellow sputum - the latter especially first thing in the morning. Treat with antibiotics: 500mg of either Ampicillin or Amoxycillin every 8 hours. The course lasts for five days, and must be completed.

Mountain Sickness (AMS):

At 5500 metres (18,000ft), or about 300 metres higher than Pangpema, atmospheric pressure is half that at sea level, and no matter how hard we breathe it is impossible to supply the same level of oxygen to the blood, and it is this deficiency that causes problems of mountain sickness - of varying degrees of seriousness.

Knowing it is possible for some mountaineers to reach the summit of Mount Everest and enjoy the view without supplementary oxygen, goes some way towards alleviating the fear of many first-time visitors to the Himalaya. Although altitude, or mountain, sickness can affect anyone, *it need not affect you*. What you need to help avoid it is to drink adequate amounts of liquid (at around 4300 metres, or 14,000ft, the body needs 3-4 litres a day), and allow sufficient time to acclimatise.

Acclimatisation is the process by which our bodies gradually adjust to altitude hypoxia - low levels of oxygen.

Individuals acclimatise at different rates, and age and level of fitness make no apparent difference. Some suffer headaches at 2500 metres (8200ft), while others can happily climb to twice that elevation without feeling discomfort other than shortness of breath. Since most of us can manage to trek to 3000 metres without experiencing any problems, it is that altitude at which one should seriously take note - not only of yourself, but of your companions. Should there be no problems at around 3000 metres, ascend another four or five hundred metres next day, and then continue to 4000 metres the day after that if there are still no signs of discomfort.

Signs to look out for are: extreme fatigue, headache and loss of appetite. Some trekkers also find they become breathless with only minimal exercise, and suffer disturbed sleep. When these symptoms develop do not go any higher until they have gone away. If they show no sign of leaving after a day or two, but instead become worse, it is important to descend to lower levels. There is no shame in this; it is not a sign of weakness and a number of trekkers (and mountaineers) each year are forced to abandon their plans to go high and retreat in the hope of returning another year. Do not take sleeping tablets or strong pain killers, as these can mask some of the symptoms.

A worsening condition is indicated by vomiting, severe headache, lack of co-ordination, wet, bubbly breathing, increased tiredness and breathlessness - even at rest. Such symptoms warn of the onset of a very serious condition which, if ignored, can lead to a loss of consciousness and death within twelve hours. The only known cure, if acted upon in time, is to *descend at once* until symptoms decrease and finally disappear completely. An improvement is usually experienced after 300 metres (1000ft) or so of descent - but the sufferer must be accompanied and should not be left alone until sufficient improvement is made in their condition.

As with all health concerns it is important to be aware of potential dangers, but keep them in perspective and not allow your concerns to devalue the pleasures of the trek. Be aware of symptoms and act upon them if and when they occur, then time permitting and energy willing, continue with your trek when signs of improvement indicate it's safe to do so.

Remember, *do not go too high too fast*.

Detailed advice may be gleaned from reading James A. Wilkerson's *Medicine for Mountaineering* (The Mountaineers), Peter Steele's *Medical Handbook for Mountaineers* (Constable) or *Altitude Illness, Prevention and Treatment* by Dr Stephen Bezruchka (The Mountaineers). A very useful little handbook entitled *The Himalayan First Aid Manual* by Jim Duff and Peter Gormly (a World Expedition Publication) is available in Kathmandu. It is a slim, lightweight publication that would fit neatly into a first aid kit.

Finally, when trekking through remote villages it is not uncommon to be approached by locals with a request for medical treatment. Advice from Nepal is to avoid the temptation to hand out medicines, for in the hills many locals will never have taken Western medicines before, and an adverse reaction may result. It is sensible not to give more than an elastoplast to villagers, and to limit medical intervention to cleansing cuts and advising them to visit the nearest clinic for further treatment if necessary.

THE FIRST AID KIT

"Anyone who is likely to find themselves more than a few hours from a hospital should consider very carefully what they need to take with them."

(Rob Ryan: *Stay Healthy Abroad*)

All trekkers, whether they are travelling in a group or alone, should

---

The trail to Gupha Pokhari, on Day 2 of the trek
from Basantpur. (Trek 1, Section 1)

Morning clouds hide the Arun Valley (Trek 1, Section 2)
For some way above Chainpur the trail has been paved (Trek 1, Section 2

carry with them a personal first aid kit, the very minimum contents being:

Elastoplast or similar dressing strips
Butterfly closures
Bandages (cotton gauze & elastic)
Throat lozenges & cough pastilles
Tincture of Iodine (in dropper bottle)
Immodium (or similar for relief of diarrhoea)
Antibiotics (Ciproxin & Ampicillin)
Rehydration solution (Dioralyte or Jeevan Jal)

Antihistamine
Emergency dental kit
Moleskin (for blisters)
Antiseptic cream
Paracetamol and/or Aspirin
Thermometer
Tiniba (to combat giardia)
Scissors
Eye drops or ointment
Safety pins

Note that most medicines, including antibiotics, are readily available without prescription in Kathmandu pharmacies.

EQUIPMENT CHECK-LIST

"I think a good deal of what we took might have come under the heading of luxuries rather than necessities, and had our subsequent transport difficulties been realised at the outset, it is safe to say that there would have been a drastic cutting down of individual and general equipment, and this without imperilling the party in any way."

(F.S. Smythe: *The Kangchenjunga Adventure*)

In a nutshell what Smythe was saying above was "sufficient is enough". While writing in his early Alpine guidebooks, Karl Baedeker put it more succinctly when he observed that "to be provided with enough and no more, may be considered the second golden rule of the traveller."

The following list should cover the requirements of most trekkers undertaking routes described in this book, and it is worth remembering that although the baggage allowance on most airlines is about 20kg (44lbs), you should aim to give your porter a kitbag to carry that is much lighter than that.

Clothing
boots & spare laces
light shoes/trainers
down jacket
fleece or sweater
shirts x 3
trekking trousers (and/or long
    skirt for women)
waterproof cagoule, poncho or
umbrella
sun hat
woollen hat/balaclava
gloves
underwear (including thermals)
socks x 3 pairs

mending kit
first aid kit
small knife
sunglasses/goggles
suncream (factor 15+) & lip salve
towel & washing kit
map & compass
whistle
toilet paper & lighter
money
passport & trek permit
boot cleaning kit
plastic bags
money belt
guidebook

Other essential items
kitbag & padlock
small rucksack
sleeping bag (4 seasons +)
sleeping bag liner
water bottle (1 litre capacity)
headtorch, batteries & bulbs

Optional
camera & lots of film
trekking poles/walking stick
binoculars
altimeter
gaiters
notebook & pens

It is useful too to have a complete change of clothes waiting at your Kathmandu hotel for use on return from trek. Most hotels have storage facilities, but make sure any baggage left behind (in a small holdall) is secure and clearly marked with your name and expected date of return.

Trekking poles have been included in the list as experience proves their value in aiding balance on stream-crossings, on trails slippery with a glaze of ice, and on steep descents where they are especially useful for anyone with problem knees. There can be no doubt that the use of trekking poles over the rough Himalayan trails can absorb a considerable amount of shock on ankles, knees and hips, and if proof were needed, studies in Germany claim that each time the pole is put to the ground it relieves the lower part of your body of between 4.5-8kg (10-18lbs) of weight. In the course of a long day's trekking, that's a lot of relief. The best poles are lightweight but strong, and are telescopic so that the length can be quickly adjusted to suit each individual's need. When reduced to their minimum length they will usually fit inside a kitbag for safe transportation on aircraft.

GETTING THERE

"Some Third World airlines which excel in in-flight service may not be so good on the ground."
(Melissa Shales [ed]: *The Traveller's Handbook*)

When booking a trek through a recognised agent in the UK, flights are usually arranged as part of the service. However, most operators offer reduced 'Land Only' costs for trekkers who, for one reason or another, prefer to make their own travel arrangements. The following notes have been compiled with this class of traveller in mind.

By Air:
International airlines currently serving Nepal from Europe are: Aeroflot, Biman Bangladesh Airlines, Pakistan International Airlines (PIA), Qatar Airways and Royal Nepal Airlines Corporation (RNAC).

Flights by Biman, PIA and Qatar Airways involve making connections in Dhaka, Karachi and Doha respectively, while Aeroflot flights from London to Kathmandu fly via Moscow. RNAC, on the other hand, operates twice weekly from London calling at Frankfurt and Dubai. RNAC flights are heavily subscribed well in advance, and anyone planning to fly with them should try booking many months before the proposed trek date. A number of mainstream airlines fly to Delhi, from where it is possible to get an onward flight to Kathmandu. The bureaucratic hassles involved in transferring from one airline to another in Delhi, however, do not make this a very attractive proposition.

Having flown many times via Bangladesh, I feel that anyone planning to do likewise should be warned that unannounced delays can result in 24 or even 48 frustrating hours being spent in Dhaka waiting for an onward flight. Over the years I have lost too many days of Himalayan trekking time kicking the dust of Dhaka's streets dreaming of snowpeaks and the peace of the hills. Lost or delayed baggage has also featured rather too often in my experience on this route. Or have I simply been unlucky?

Return flights out of Kathmandu are heavily booked during the main trekking seasons, and it is absolutely essential to reconfirm your homeward flight at least 72 hours before departure time. Check with your agent that this is being done on your behalf. If not, make sure you do it yourself. Failure to do so may lead to the loss of your seat, regardless of the fact that you have a valid ticket. The best bet is to reconfirm before you even set out on trek. Then your conscience should be clear.

Before spending the last of your Nepalese currency, check the amount of departure tax that has to be paid at the airport. The precise amount depends on your next destination.

By Other Means:
Travellers heading for Nepal from India will find that a combination of road and rail travel may take as much as three days for the journey from Delhi to Kathmandu by way of Agra, Varanasi, Patna and Nepal's busiest border crossing at Birganj. Coming from Darjeeling it is possible to take a train to Siliguri, and taxi from there to the border post at Kakarbitta in the eastern Terai, which is linked with the capital by daily buses.

Travel Within Nepal:
The journey from Kathmandu to the start of the Kangchenjunga trek will either be a) by bus to Basantpur (a $1^1/_2$-2 day ride), b) flight to Biratnagar followed by bus ride to Basantpur, c) flight to Tumlingtar or d) flight to Taplejung (Suketar) - depending on the duration of the trip. Travel will be arranged by your trekking agent.

PERMITS AND VISAS

"Trekking permit should keep along with the trekker while trekking."
(Department of Immigration, H.M. Government)

Apart from Indian nationals, all foreign visitors to Nepal need a valid passport and a tourist visa. The latter can be obtained on arrival at Tribhuvan International Airport, Kathmandu, and currently costs $25 which must be paid for in dollar bills. You'll need a passport photograph too. Visa regulations and costs are subject to frequent changes, but at present these are valid initially for a thirty day period. If you plan to stay in Nepal for a longer period, a visa extension can be arranged at the Central Immigration Office on Tridevi Marg, between Kantipath and Thamel. The maximum continuous period allowed for a visit to Nepal is currently 90 days.

Having a visa in your passport does not allow unrestricted travel throughout Nepal, and in order to travel beyond the Kathmandu Valley, Pokhara and Chitwan National Park requires a trekking permit (whether or not you intend to trek) issued by the Department of Immigration. The permit lists the names of villages on the agreed route, and will be checked at various police posts along the trail where details are entered in an official leger. Permits for Kangchenjunga are only issued to fully-equipped parties travelling under the aegis of a recognised trekking agent, and will normally be obtained on behalf of group members. You will need two passport-size photos - instant passport photo facilities are situated near the Immigration Office, should you forget to bring some from home.

Whilst permit applications and fees will usually be taken care of by the organising company or Kathmandu agent, each member of the trekking party should be aware of the rules and regulations printed on the back of the trekking permit. These are summarised below:

1: Trekkers should keep their permits with them throughout the trek. (However, some Sirdars prefer to look after these, and deal with check-post formalities on behalf of their clients.)

2: Permits must be shown on demand to Immigration or Police authorities.

3: Trekkers are not allowed to trek in areas previously notified as restricted.

4: Permits should be surrendered at either the Immigration Department or port of exit, on completion of the trek. (I have yet to meet anyone who has complied with this ruling, as trekking permits are invariably taken home as personal souvenirs!)

5: Deviation from the prescribed routes noted on the permit will be treated as a violation of law.

6: Environmental rules for trekking are summarised as follows:

- Protect the natural environment.
- Leave campsites cleaner than you found them.
- Limit deforestation by making no wood fires.
- Burn dry papers and packets in a safe place.
- Keep water sources clean and avoid using pollutants.
- Plants should be left to flourish in their natural habitats.

- Help your guides and porters to follow conservation measures.

7: Respect local traditions, protect local cultures, maintain local pride:

- When taking photographs respect privacy.
- Respect religious sites and artefacts.
- Do not give money or other gifts to children since this will encourage begging.
- Respect for local etiquette earns you respect.

8: Filming in restricted or notified areas without permission is strictly forbidden.

ENVIRONMENTAL CONSIDERATIONS

"Returning through Sikkim [in 1938] I happened to visit the base camp on the Zemu glacier used by the Germans for their two attempts on Kangchenjunga; the amount of rubbish strewn about was reminiscent of the day after a Bank Holiday at one of England's more popular beauty spots."

(H.W. Tilman: *Everest 1938*)

Rubbish disposal:
Perhaps it is no bad thing to be reminded by Tilman that litter in the Himalaya is not a recent phenomenon brought about by large numbers of trekkers, but something that our predecessors were guilty of too. That's not to say we should be complacent and uncaring, but that a background of neglect needs to be addressed. If you turn up at a campsite previously used by others and find rubbish left lying about, or a *charpi* (latrine) hole not completely filled in, your experience will be devalued and you'll feel justifiably miffed. So make sure you are not guilty of the same failing when you leave next day. Litter is unacceptable wherever it is found, so please be considerate throughout your time in Nepal.

Himalayan hillfolk have no cultural background of rubbish disposal, for until the advent of plastics, tin and glass, there was no real problem. All waste was biodegradable. But now locals, trekkers and mountaineering expeditions alike carry huge amounts of non-degradable goods into the mountains - much of which will need to be disposed of eventually. Consider this: it has been estimated that a group of 15 trekkers generates about 24kg (52lbs) of non-burnable, non-degradable rubbish in the course of a two-week trek. Add to that natural body waste, toilet and tissue paper, and the scale of the problem may be imagined.

It is the duty of everyone to dispose of their own rubbish in a considerate manner. When trekking in a group your leader should arrange for communal non-burnable waste to be collected in plastic bags and carried out. But individuals ought to do the same with their own personal items - used foil medicine strips, dead batteries etc - which could easily be carried home at the end of the trek. Wendy Brewer Lama, in the booklet *Trekking Gently in the Himalaya*, estimates that nearly a quarter of a million torch (flashlight) batteries are used by trekkers each year, and as Nepal has no proper means for disposing of them properly, all used batteries should be taken home for safe disposal, while burnables can be gathered together and destroyed in a common pit at the campsite, making sure that no paper or cardboard is left to blow away or be dug up by animals.

As for toilet demands, on group treks the toilet tent should be sited at least 50 metres (150ft) from water sources, the hole deep enough to meet the needs of the group and a square of turf kept to one side for replacing later. Burn your own toilet paper after use and sprinkle a little dirt in the hole to discourage flies, and ensure the pit is properly filled in and covered before leaving the campsite.

Should you be caught out along the trail, as is likely to happen at some time or other, choose your site with care, dig a hole with a small trowel or penknife, and fill it in afterwards. Again, do not forget to burn used toilet paper. Tampons and sanitary towels should be wrapped well and carried until they can be disposed of in the next latrine pit.

Don't pollute the water:
Streams and rivers are often the only source of drinking water for hill villages in the Himalaya, so it is important to avoid polluting them. When bathing or washing clothes use a small bowl borrowed from the kitchen crew, and dispose of the soapy waste well away from any natural water source. If possible, bring biodegradable soap from home.

Fuel-efficient trekking:
Throughout your trek to Kangchenjunga all meals should be prepared and water heated using kerosene stoves rather than wood fires. Only the 'greenest' and most eco-friendly of trekking agents provide cooking fuel for porters, but by supplying warm clothing and shelter for all trek staff at high altitudes, the amount of firewood cut down can be limited. Campfires should be outlawed where timber is in obvious short supply.

Keep off the crops:
Out of the high mountains trekking routes described within these pages lead through terraced farmland. Some of the trails wind alongside irrigation channels on bare-earth dikes and around the

edges of planted fields. Please take care not to damage crops, dikes or walls, and close all gates behind you.

CULTURAL INTERACTION

"Try not to fume or be frustrated by inexplicable behaviour or situations that cause delay. You are part of the dance and can't always change its tempo."
(Hugh Swift: *Trekking in Nepal, West Tibet and Bhutan*)

The environmental impact on the Nepalese landscape made by trekkers and a growing number of mountaineering expeditions has been well documented, although some of the publicity has been rather wide of the mark. What has not been so clearly noted, however, is the negative effect Western attitudes can have on Nepali culture, and it is unfortunate that few commercial trekking agents in the West provide any guidance on the mode of dress or behaviour their clients should adopt when travelling there. It is no use viewing the host nation as backward and living in the Middle Ages, or that it's high time it was dragged into the 21st century. As it's our choice to go there, we have a duty to fit in with Nepal's cultural heritage, to respect the beliefs of its people and to be part of the dance, as Hugh Swift would have it, and not attempt to change its tempo.

When it comes to cross-cultural interaction, most of us are innocents abroad, and it is sometimes possible to cause offence in the most innocent of ways - although Nepalis are such warm-hearted hosts that they will rarely reveal their displeasure. The oft-quoted maxim 'Nepal is there to change you, not for you to change Nepal' is worth remembering, in Kathmandu and throughout the trek.

The following guidelines are offered as a form of cultural code, which may help both in the planning of your trip, and from day to day on the trail.

Affection: Avoid public displays of affection. Kissing, cuddling and holding hands in public are frowned upon by locals.

Begging: In general don't encourage it. Children who ask for school pens, balloons, sweets or money should be discouraged, for aiding them to become beggars will inevitably destroy their self-respect. On the other hand, donations to schools, health centres or other worthwhile community projects, will help Nepalis to help themselves.

Dress: Be modestly clad. A state of undress is unacceptable in both sexes. Men should not bare their chests in public, nor should women wear revealing blouses. Tight-fitting clothes should be avoided, and women are advised to choose either a long skirt or slacks - never shorts.

Food: Do not touch food or utensils to be used by Nepalis. Never give or take food with the left hand, and if cutlery is unavailable, only use your right hand to eat with. When giving or receiving gifts it is considered polite to use both hands.

Haggling: In Kathmandu haggling is part of the trade culture, but on trek things are a little different. In teahouses pay the going rate for drinks, biscuits etc. If you're after a locally-made rug, or other souvenir that's offered, be prepared to haggle again. If in doubt, ask your trek leader for advice.

The hearth: Sometimes you may be invited into a village house. Be aware that many hillfolk consider the hearth as sacred, so never discard rubbish into your host's fire, no matter how small or insignificant it may seem. Nor should you sit next to the fire in a Nepali home unless specifically invited to do so.

Legs & feet: Soles of the feet should not be pointed at a Nepali, nor should legs be so outstretched that they need to be stepped over. Feet are considered unclean.

Monasteries: When visiting monasteries always remove boots or shoes before entering, and make a donation before leaving. In respect to local culture and belief, please refrain from smoking or noisy behaviour in or near a sacred site.

Photography: Be discreet when taking photographs of local people. Try to imagine how you'd react at home if a total stranger pushed a 55mm lens into your granny's face. Take time to establish a relationship with your potential subject, and ask permission before taking their photograph - and respect their right to say no. And please don't promise to send a copy of the photo you've taken unless you're certain to fulfil that promise.

Prayer walls: Always pass to the left of a prayer wall (mani wall), chorten or stupa.

Short-cuts: Stick to trails and avoid trampling plants. Taking short-cuts can add to problems of soil erosion. Avoid walking through fields where crops are growing, and should you be faced by oncoming animals on the trail, make sure they pass on the downhill side.

Smile: A smile is multi-lingual. Be patient and friendly towards local people. Nepalis smile a lot, and that warmth ought to be reflected back.

Touch: Never touch a Nepali on the head, and do not touch anyone with your shoes. Pointing with your finger is considered rude; instead use your right hand extended, with fingers together.

Wealth: Be discreet when handling money, and avoid tempting locals to envy by making an obvious display of the contents of your wallet. Keep a few small denomination rupee notes handy for buying tea along the trail. Don't leave valuables unattended.

Finally, the word *Namaste*, given with palms pressed together in an attitude of prayer, is the universal greeting of Nepal. It means "I salute the god within you" and will be well received when offered in villages or teahouses along the trail. Use it with a smile - and mean it, for you are offering a sign of respect. From such simple beginnings may grow a flower of understanding.

MAPS

"The adventurous trekker has much to be thankful for when it comes to maps of Nepal, for much is left to the imagination."
(Bill O'Connor: *Adventure Treks - Nepal*)

The Kangchenjunga region is covered by several maps available in Kathmandu, some of which are also obtainable in the UK. Bill O'Connor's comment quoted above is true in regard to most of these, although for trekking purposes they are good enough. Names of villages, rivers and mountain peaks occasionally vary from one sheet to another, and different ways of spelling the same features abound.

Most sheets available are based on the Survey of India, dating from the 1920s, and have been redrawn at a different scale with some imagination. And when you bear in mind that the contour lines on some of these are spaced at 500 metre (1640ft) intervals, you'll understand that a true picture of the country you're wandering through should not be expected.

The three maps most easily found in Kathmandu that cover the region described in this guide are as follows:

1: Mandala Productions 'Latest Trekking Map' *Dhankuta to Kanchenjunga, Mt Everest, Makalu & Arun Valley*. This blue dyeline sheet is drawn to a scale of 1:192,500 with 500 metre contours. Altitude measurements are suspect and distances between villages questionable. Useful for general plotting of the route before you go, but note that sections of trail along the Tamur River are shown on the wrong bank, as is the village of Kyapra (Gyapra) between Amjilassa and Ghunsa.

2: Mandala Maps *Kangchenjunga Makalu* at 1:225,000 scale. Contours on this sheet are spaced at 250 metre intervals, main trekking routes are marked in solid red lines and, in common with the above-mentioned map, the route along the Tamur River is inaccurately marked. In addition the cartographer has conjured up a few villages that do not exist in reality. Again, distances given between some villages are pure fantasy.

3: Nepa Maps *Kangchenjunga*, drawn by Paolo Gondoni at a scale of 1:175,000. This is the most attractive of those readily available and, for everyday use, the most useful. It still contains plenty of errors, though, and with contours at 250 metre intervals, fails to provide any meaningful idea of the trek's countless undulations. It also fails to show the important trail to Suketar airstrip above Taplejung.

A more accurate series of maps, surveyed by the Finnish Government aid organisation during 1992-95, and published in 1997 by HMG Survey of Nepal under the heading 'Finnmap', covers the Kangchenjunga region at 1:50,000. Unfortunately at the time of writing these have not yet become available, either in Kathmandu or in the UK. Cordee, the mountain map and book specialists of 3a

De Montfort Street, Leicester LE1 7HD, plan to stock these as soon as they are available. It is probable that about four sheets will be needed to cover the same area contained in the above-mentioned maps.

NEPAL - FACTS AND FIGURES

"Nepal is a country of such wonderful variety that even the Nepalese themselves have not yet had time to explore the richness of their own heritage."

(David L. Snellgrove: *Himalayan Pilgrimage*)

Few visitors to this magical Himalayan kingdom will come away without discovering that there is much more to Nepal than mountains - despite the fact that it contains the largest number of the world's 8000 metre (26,000ft) peaks, and it will be mountains that draw you to the country in the first place. It is, as David Snellgrove said, a country of wonderful variety; rectangular in shape and measuring roughly 800 by 240 kilometres (500 x 150 miles), bordered in the north by Tibet (China), and elsewhere by India.

In the south lies the tropical belt of the **Terai**, in effect an extension of the Gangetic plain; a steamy, once-malarial region of jungle, now transformed into a productive agricultural lowland, with few towns and practically no commercialism outside Chitwan National Park.

On the northern edge of the Terai green foothills fold into the broad **central region**. This consists of fertile hills rising in altitude from 600 to 2000 metres (2000-6500ft), and includes the sub-tropical Kathmandu Valley and neighbouring valley basins. The Kathmandu Valley was once filled by a lake formed by the uplifting Mahabharat range, which effectively blocked its south-flowing rivers. Until the mid 18th century, this *was* Nepal, with three sovereign kingdoms ruled by the Malla dynasty, while today it is very much the heart of the country fully unified by Prithvi Narayan Shah in 1768, the springboard from which so many mountain adventures begin.

The **Himalaya** forms only the northern part of the country, the highest mountains being largely 'protected' from the foothills by a series of deep river-cut gorges which effectively create demarcation zones of vegetation. Only the highest reaches of the most remote valleys remain uninhabited, and one of the delights of trekking here is to be found in travelling through the villages of an ethnically diverse population.

Nepal is the world's only Hindu monarchy. Official statistics suggest that in a population of around 20 million, some 89.5% claim to be Hindu, and just 5.3% practise Buddhism. But with a long history of religious tolerance, **Hindu** and **Buddhist** co-exist in harmony, and merge compatibly in so many different ways that it is not always easy to separate them. There may be Buddhist prayer flags flying over a Hindu temple, and Hindu gods sharing Buddhist sites. Kathmandu is full of sacred sites, most of which are Hindu, of course, yet the deeper you get into the mountains, so Buddhism takes over as the dominant religion, and chortens, prayer flags, mani walls and simple gompas (monasteries) provide a constant reminder of a tradition of spirituality encountered within the shadow of the highest peaks.

The official **language**, Nepali, is derived from Pahori which comes from northern India and is spoken by some 58% of the population. But it has been said that there are as many different languages as there are races, and as many dialects as there are villages. In the Kathmandu Valley the original language of Newari uses no less than three different alphabets. Fortunately for the Western trekker English is widely understood, not only in Kathmandu, but in many villages along the more popular trails and among senior members of the trek crew. But the effort taken to learn a few Nepali words and phrases will be more than repaid. A brief glossary will be found in Appendix D.

Although Nepal numbers among the world's **poorest nations** in terms of per capita income, the visitor here does not experience the same sense of hopeless poverty that is so prevalent in a number of other Eastern countries. The majority of the population (over 80%) depend for their livelihood on **agriculture**, much of which is subsistence farming on the intricate terraced fields of the hill country. Something like 17% of land is under cultivation, and about 30% covered in forest. However, the demands of a fast-growing population (an annual rise of 2.1%) and a corresponding increase in livestock have changed Nepal from being a net exporter of food to a net importer. Year by year the food deficit is widening as productivity is declining, and there is a marked reduction too in forests that needs to be arrested. Nepal now faces serious economic and environmental problems which only considered development can address.

Foreign development projects continue to pour money into the country, but a number of these schemes are of questionable value. In his book *Travels in Nepal*, Charlie Pye-Smith provides an interesting commentary on the question of **foreign aid**, and *The Rough Guide to Nepal* also includes one or two sobering articles that are worth reading by anyone interested in the question of development aid.

Tourism continues to be the largest source of earned income, although only 2% of the population find active employment in it. Trekking, of course, forms an important part of the tourist industry and provides much-needed foreign currency, although a large slice of the money paid for a group trek organised by many Western agencies never reaches Nepal.

International **telecommunication** links are made possible through the British earth satellite station installed in 1982. Telephone connections with Europe and the United States are good, and are widely available in Kathmandu where a number of small offices offering telephone, telex and fax facilities are to be found in Thamel and other tourist haunts (look for signs emblazoned with the initials: ISD/STD/IDD). Most hotels and trekking agencies in the capital are now accessible by fax.

Nepalese **time** is 5 hours 45 minutes ahead of GMT (15 minutes ahead of Indian Standard Time), 12 hours 45 minutes ahead of New York, 15 hours 45 minutes ahead of Los Angeles, and 21 hours 45 minutes ahead of Sydney, Australia.

The **General Post Office** (GPO) in Kathmandu is located at the junction of Kantipath and Kicha-Pokhari Road. The office is open daily, except Saturdays and public holidays, from 10.00 to 17.00 (16.00 November to February). When posting letters, cards or packages, always ensure that stamps are franked by the counter clerk. There is invariably a queue at the special counter reserved for this. Some reliable Kathmandu hotels and guest houses will take mail to the post office for you. Expect letters and postcards to take anything upwards of ten days to be delivered, but do not mail anything in a public postbox if you want it to reach its destination.

Poste Restante facilities are available at the GPO, and are quite efficient. Send post with the recipient's name clearly marked, and with the surname underlined or printed in capital letters, c/o Poste Restante, GPO, Kathmandu, Nepal. The Poste Restante facility is a self-service affair. In a room set aside for this, mail is filed alphabetically in large trays where you help yourself. Mail is usually held for around two months.

The local **currency** is the Rupee (Rps) which consists of 100 Paisa. As a 'soft' currency it has no exchange value outside Nepal, and should not be taken out of the country. Travellers' cheques and 'hard' currencies can be exchanged at Tribhuvan International Airport on arrival, and at various banks which are open daily except Saturdays, from 10.00 until about 14.00. Hotels will usually change dollar bills too. Always collect your exchange receipts as these may be needed when applying for trek permits or visa extensions (regulations change with some frequency), and will also be required if you need to reconvert unspent Rupees at the end of your trip. Make a point of accumulating plenty of small denomination notes for use on trek. Notes are in the following categories: 1, 2, 5, 10, 20, 50, 100, 500 and 1000 Rps. There are also coins to the value of 1, 2, and 5 Rps. In Kathmandu major credit cards are growing in acceptance, but these, of course, are useless in the hills.

TIME IN KATHMANDU

"There are ... a thousand Kathmandus, layered and dovetailed and piled on top of one another in an extravagant morass of misery, chaos and dignity."

(David Reed: *The Rough Guide to Nepal*)

David Reed is right. There are a thousand Kathmandus, for it's a true conundrum of a city with insufficient answers to too many questions. The world-weary traveller who sees through the trappings of tourism may find his time there dominated by the misery of the East. The new-arrival, whose first experience of the Third World this is, will no doubt be appalled at the apparent chaos of the city,

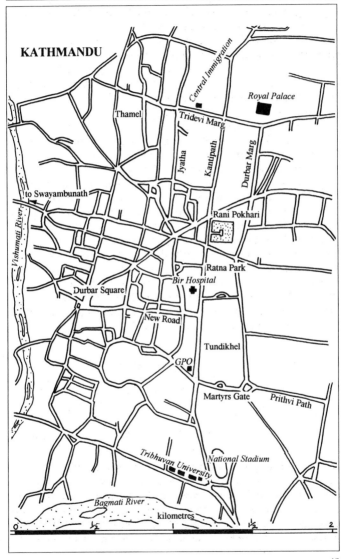

KATHMANDU

Central Immigration

Royal Palace

Thamel

Tridevi Marg

Jyatha

Kantipath

Durbar Marg

to Swayambunath

Vishumati River

Rani Pokhari

Ratna Park

Bir Hospital

Durbar Square

New Road

Tundikhel

GPO

Martyrs Gate

Prithvi Path

Tribhuvan University

National Stadium

Bagmati River

kilometres

0   ½   1   1½   2

while to the romantic it will be the dignity of Kathmandu that shines through.

Despite all the obvious disadvantages and seemingly insoluble problems of an Eastern capital growing too fast for its own good, it remains one of the world's most magical cities, and a few days spent there either before or after trek, will be rewarding for most. The city has a unique atmosphere, a wealth of fascinating buildings, a cultural heritage that would take a lifetime to fully unravel, and a scene worthy of examination at every corner. And after weeks spent among the mountains, it is a great place to sample a change of menu, for there are dozens of inexpensive restaurants to satisfy all appetites. There are numerous hotels and guest houses of varying degrees of comfort, and enough shops and street traders offering a thousand and one 'bargains' to help you spend the last of your money.

Kathmandu's hotels range from the fancy and comparatively high-priced, such as those on Durbar Marg - Hotel Sherpa with its floor shows, Hotel de l'Annapurna with its sauna and swimming pool, and the Yak and Yeti with its opulent restaurants - to an array of unpretentious lodgings for the budget-conscious stuffed away in Thamel back streets or on the one-time hippy hideout of Freak Street (Jhochhen Tol) on the south side of Durbar Square. Popular middle of the range accommodation includes the perennial favourite of the Kathmandu Guest House in the heart of Thamel, the Norbhu Linkha off Bhagabati Bahal, and Mustang Holiday Inn hidden round the back of Jyatha. Jyatha is lined with numerous medium- and low-priced hotels sought out mostly by independent travellers, while the Yellow Pagoda beside the busy Kantipath is often taken over by trekking parties from the U.K.

For a thousand years and more Kathmandu profited from control of the main trade route between India and Tibet, taxes from this trade financing Newari artisans whose craftsmanship gave Kathmandu and its neighbouring cities their architectural elegance. Rimmed with hills and encircled by rivers the city, badly damaged by earthquake on 15 January 1934, draws ever-larger numbers of the population from the outlying hills, for as is common throughout the developing world, there are those who imagine the streets of the capital to be paved with gold. But Kathmandu suffers from traffic pollution, an inadequate water supply, unreliable electricity and no proper underground sewage system. In the 1870s David Wright, a surgeon at the British Residency, produced a report which cynics might consider apt today. It read "The streets of Kathmandu are very narrow, mere lanes in fact; and the whole town is very dirty ... In short, from a sanitary point of view, Kathmandu may be said to be built on a dunghill in the middle of latrines."

That is but one view, just one of the thousand Kathmandus. What else? Well, the city is a cornucopia of colour, of smells, of noise. It *is* dirty. But it's also exciting, vibrant, lively. A dull cloud of pollution hangs over the valley, yet below it there is often unrestrained gaiety. In countless streets medieval buildings are adorned with carvings of delicate and timeless beauty. There are people everywhere, the narrow alleyways and broad modern streets acrush with humanity. Traffic streams in an endless honking procession through the daylight hours along the main highways. Bicycle rickshaws, motor-bikes, tempos and taxis bounce and weave through the teeming streets of Thamel, and manage somehow to avoid collision with crowds of traders, bustling porters, tourists and beggars - and the occasional cow.

Thamel is the ever-popular tourist district in the north-west of the city. It is a brazen mish-mash of building styles, curiously-worded hoardings, hash-touting wide boys, carpet salesmen, flute sellers and bleary-eyed world travellers - a hybrid receptive to the latest whim. Go away for a year, and on return you'll find an old familiar shop or restaurant gone and a new building in its place. Thamel is not representative of Kathmandu, only of itself. Nepal it is not. It has become a parody; refreshing in many ways, appalling in others. But there's still plenty of budget accommodation around and a fine selection of restaurants and cheap Western-style cafés and drinking haunts with thumping music where travellers behave just as they do in the West. There are bookshops, suppliers of climbing and trekking equipment, a specialist trekker's food store, and outfitters of every kind. Should your airline redirect your baggage by mistake, you will find all you need in the shop-lined streets of Thamel. (Note: if the nightmare does happen and your baggage fails to arrive in Kathmandu, you can rent down jackets and good sleeping bags for a very modest sum from a number of outdoor gear shops.)

But it is the wealth of religious and cultural sites that puts Kathmandu in a category all its own and makes the town so appealing. "There are nearly as many temples as houses, and as many idols as inhabitants," wrote William Kirkpatrick in 1811, and while there are certainly more houses and inhabitants today, there is no shortage of places to visit, either in the capital itself, or in the neighbouring towns of Patan and Bhaktapur, and throughout the Kathmandu Valley. The following suggestions merely scratch the surface. For more detailed information, background history and as a pointer to the full glories of the valley, the *Insight Guide to Nepal* is highly recommended.

Kathmandu:
Durbar Square is a must, and is the obvious place from which to begin an exploration of the city, for it contains more than fifty important monuments, shrines and temples, as well as the huge one-time Royal Palace, and the home of the Kumari, the living goddess, providing a superb roofscape of exotic shapes. Intricate carvings adorn every building; erotic figures, patterns and religious symbols have been delicately etched on practically every strut and beam, and around each doorway and window, by generations of Newari craftsmen. Early morning is the best time to visit. Street vendors are setting out their wares, porters gather to await employment, the faithful scurry to various temples for their first devotions of the day, and the place comes alive with streams of light, colour and movement. By mid-morning the Square is crowded, and nearby row upon row of identical kukri knives, carved Buddhas and bangles, stretch from one end to the other between the Kumari Chowk and Freak Street - the ultimate flea market.

To the north of Durbar Square, midway between the Square and Thamel, and secluded off the busy street of Shukrapath, stands the biggest stupa of central Kathmandu. **Kathesimbhu** is a colourful gathering place for Buddhist monks, tourists and the children of a neighbouring school who use the surrounding space as a playground. There's another stupa, a low modest one, standing in a square to the north of this, with street traders squatting among their wares at its base.

The stupa of **Swayambhunath** overlooks the city from its lofty

The stupa at Swayambhunath gazes over Kathmandu

hilltop perch above the Vishumati River which flows round the western fringe of Kathmandu. A long flight of some 300 stone steps leads among trees where monkeys play, passing trinket sellers, beggars and snake charmers, to reach the stupa where Buddha's eyes gaze out across the valley. Prayer wheels encircle the great white dome, and behind it an active gompa attracts visitors. Inside hundreds of butter lamps flicker while drums, gongs and trumpets accompany each devotion. Again, go early in the morning and watch sunrise, and as you do you'll be accompanied by musicians and chanting devotees beginning the day with prayer.

While the Vishumati flows round the western side of Kathmandu, the Bagmati twists along the eastern boundary and, not far from the airport, is straddled by **Pashupatinath**, the most important Hindu site in all Nepal. Hundreds of devout Hindus gather there day by day, and ritual bathing takes place in the fetid waters of this sacred river. Entrance to the main temple complex is forbidden to non-Hindus, but on the east bank a series of terraces lined with identical *chaityas* (like small stupas in appearance) provides a good viewpoint from which to study not only the gilded temple opposite, but also riverside activities below. In the river itself women do their laundry, while Hindus approaching death are carried from the nearby *dharmsalas* (rest houses) and lain on stone slabs with their feet in the water until all life has drained from them. Nearby ghats are used for cremation, the ceremonies carried out in full public view. When these are being performed, tourists should act with sensitivity, and avoid intruding with prying eyes and cameras.

North-east of Kathmandu, and a little north of Pashupatinath, the great Buddhist stupa of **Bodhnath** (Bauddha or Boudhanath) is one of the world's largest, its huge dome, which measures 40 metres (130ft) in height, being seen from afar and marking the centre of Tibetan culture in Nepal. All four orders of Tibetan Buddhism are represented in the many monasteries that surround the stupa. Non-Buddhist visitors are welcome to enter these buildings, but shoes should be removed before entering, and permission sought before taking any photographs. One of the best places from which to view the site is from the rooftop restaurant, Stupa View - especially at evening time.

Patan:

South of Kathmandu, and separated from it only by the Bagmati River, the once-independent kingdom of Patan (Lalitpur) was founded, it is claimed, in the third century BC by the emperor Ashoka and his daughter Carumati. Primarily a Buddhist town it boasts around 150 former monasteries, but there are also many Hindu temples and shrines and scores of exotic secular buildings, so that it would take weeks of concentrated study to visit each one in detail.

This 'town of a thousand golden roofs' has its own **Durbar Square** with the former Royal Palace facing a complex of Newari-crafted architectural gems. The Palace itself has three main courtyards open to the public, each one displaying the skills of generations of woodcarvers. The nearby **Kwa Bahal** (or Golden Temple) dates from the 12th century and, with its ornate statues and gilded roofs, is worth seeking out - please remove footwear before stepping into the lower courtyard.

Jawalakhel, on the south-western edge of Patan, is where many Tibetans have settled following the Chinese invasion of their country in the 1950s. A thriving carpet factory has been established there which is usually on the itinerary of busloads of tourists.

Like Kathmandu, Patan is a bustling town with a vibrancy all its own. A town of artisans, metalwork is a speciality, the narrow alleys and side streets ringing to the sound of hammer or file on copper and tin. Once you've absorbed as much spiritual and architectural delight as you can manage, it is worth strolling round the tiny workshops where local craftsmen pick out ornamental filigree with hammer and punch, or spend an hour or so haggling in the bazaar with the street vendors.

Bhaktapur:

Also known by its former name of Bhadgaon, this handsome restored town lies 16 kilometres (10 miles) to the east of Kathmandu. Described by Percival Landon as "willingly remote from her neighbours, and one of the most picturesque towns in the East", it is reached through open country before the road climbs among pine trees and alongside two small reservoirs on the outskirts of the town itself. Bhaktapur is reached by frequent trolley bus service from Kathmandu, and passengers are dropped about ten minutes' walk south of town. A taxi ride from Kathmandu is less ethnic and more expensive (but still cheap by Western standards), and you can be dropped right at the gateway to Durbar Square.

This perfectly preserved medieval city has joined the 'fleece the tourist' brigade, and visitors now have to pay a fee before passing through the gateway on the west side of town. On each of my last three visits the cost of entry had doubled.

Badly damaged in the 1934 earthquake that devastated Kathmandu, Bhaktapur nevertheless retains much of its medieval character and is well worth giving a day to explore. Some of the best will be seen on entering **Durbar Square** which forms a broad and open approach to a magnificent collection of temples and monuments. At least two large temples in the Square were completely destroyed in the earthquake, but those that remain are set out with sufficient space to enable the visitor to study them from different angles without being confused among other crowded buildings.

Whilst Durbar Square is the main focus of attention, a short 100 metre stroll down a narrow street cutting away from the south-eastern corner leads to **Taumadhi Tol**, a smaller but more lively square surrounded by lovely old Newari houses and dominated by the pagoda-like **Nyatapola**, Bhaktapur's tallest temple, which dates from 1702 and stands on a five-stepped pedestal guarded by a succession of stone wrestlers, elephants, lions, griffins and goddesses. A fine view of this, and the rest of the square, may be obtained from the balconies of Café Nyatapola, itself a delightful building.

The oldest part of town lies to the east of Durbar Square. Here **Tachapol Tol** (Dattatraya Square) has two old, but not particularly elaborate, temples, and a slender pillar-statue of Garud. Linked to the rest of town by narrow alleyways, there is much to explore in Tachapol Tol. Take special note of the magnificent carvings that adorn so many buildings, especially around the windows and doorways of the 18th century **Pujari Math** where the lattice-work of the famed **Peacock Window** is perhaps the most celebrated piece of woodwork in the Kathmandu Valley. The art of the woodcarver here has reached the very peak of perfection.

Dhulikhel:
This small and well-preserved town nestles in a saddle of hills about 30 kilometres (19 miles) east of Kathmandu at an altitude of about

Autumn ploughing in the foothill country below Gurja

1550 metres (5085ft). There are several hotels catering for tourists who visit in order to enjoy the splendour of a Himalayan sunrise. For the best views you'll have to walk for about 45 minutes or so south-east of the town to gain the summit of a 1715 metre (5627ft) hill. From there a splendid panorama stretches from Annapurna to Everest, with Langtang and Helambu forming the central part of the view.

Nagarkot:
Probably the best-known 'resort' on the rim of the Kathmandu Valley, Nagarkot lies about 15 kilometres (9 miles) north-east of Bhaktapur, and is served by tourist minibus from the capital and by public bus from Bhaktapur. As with Dhulikhel, sunrise and sunset views of the mountains are quite magical, although unlike Dhulikhel you can enjoy a classic panorama virtually from your hotel window. There is no real village, as such, at Nagarkot, just a scattering of hotels along a ridge. Postcard and hotel touts who latch on the moment you arrive can be rather wearing. Once clear of them, however, it can be a relaxing place after the bustle of Kathmandu. The air is much cleaner too; a useful place to escape to for a day or so, and there are some pleasant low-level treks to be had in the nearby hills. You could also walk back down to Kathmandu via Bhaktapur.

✻　✻　✻

THE TREKS

"...the exploration of unknown peaks, glaciers and valleys, the finding and crossing of new passes to connect one area with another, is the most fascinating occupation I know. The variety of experience, the constantly changing scene, the gradual unfolding of the geography of the range are deeply satisfying, for they yield a very real understanding, almost a sense of personal possession, of the country explored."

(Eric Shipton)

TABLE OF ROUTE SUMMARIES

Route	Distance	Height gain/loss	Time	Page
Trek 1: Kangchenjunga North Base Camp				
Kathmandu to Basantpur and the Trek to Dobhan				
Basantpur - Door Pani - Chauki	16km	+590m/-240m	3½-4hrs	68
Chauki - Buje Deorali	12km	+365m/-205m	5hrs	70
Buje Deorali - Gurja - Dobhan	12km	-2060m	5hrs	73
Tumlingtar to Dobhan				
Tumlingtar - Chainpur	14km	+878m	4½-5hrs	78
Chainpur - Chitlang	13km	+255m	3½-4hrs	80
Chitlang - Milke Danda	9km	+1740+m/-600m	5-5½hrs	81
Milke Danda - Dobhan	13km	-1740m	4-4½hrs	82
Dobhan to Pangpema				
Dobhan - Mitlung	12km	+235m	3½-4hrs	84
Mitlung - Sinwa - Chirwa	11km	+435m	4-4½hrs	88
Chirwa - Tapethok - Sokathum	11km	+405m	4hrs	90
Sokathum - Amjilassa	9km	+910m	4hrs	92
Amjilassa - Gyapra	8km	+200m	3-3½hrs	94
Gyapra - Phole - Ghunsa	9km	+750m	4hrs	96

※　※　※

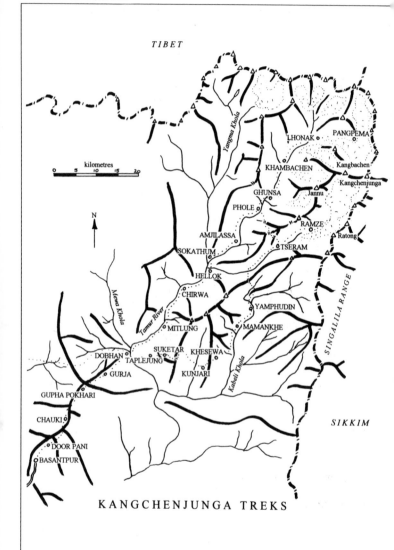

TIBET

kilometres
0 5 10 15 20

N

LHONAK
PANGPEMA
KHAMBACHEN
Kangbachen
Kangchenjunga
GHUNSA
Jannu
PHOLE
AMJILASSA
RAMZE
SOKATHUM
TSERAM
Ratong
HELLOK
CHIRWA
YAMPHUDIN
Mewa Khola
Tamur River
MITLUNG
MAMANKHE
SUKETAR
DOBHAN
KHESEWA
TAPLEJUNG
Kabeli Khola
GURJA
KUNJARI
GUPHA POKHARI
SINGALILA RANGE
CHAUKI
SIKKIM
DOOR PANI
BASANTPUR

KANGCHENJUNGA TREKS

✓ see p 90

TREK 1:
KANGCHENJUNGA
NORTH BASE CAMP

"Mentally, a man is lost in this country. Like an astronomer he can estimate distance only in figures. His brain is too small, too tied to the little houses, towns, villages, and hedgerows among which he is accustomed to live, to grasp the real magnitude of these immense landscapes."

(F.S. Smythe: *The Kangchenjunga Adventure*)

As was noted in the Introduction, early explorers of the Kangchenjunga range concentrated on the Sikkim flank, and even when they managed to visit the Nepalese valleys, their approach invariably began in Darjeeling and crossed into Nepal via the Singalila Ridge. It was only in the second half of the 20th century that mountaineers took to the old trails of communication that scored across the Nepalese foothills above the bazaar town of Dharan as a way of gaining access to Kangchenjunga, the route of which has since become the regular approach for trekkers.

Beginning in the foothill country between the valleys of the Arun and Tamur, the trek to the base camp area of Pangpema, on the north-west side of Kangchenjunga, provides all the scenic drama and variety that symbolize the trekking experience in Nepal. You begin in balmy warmth among vegetated hills, and make steady progress towards distant snows that hang among the clouds. For a few days the immense landscapes hinted at by Smythe seem almost overwhelming - can it be possible that in less than two weeks' time you will be on the far side of that ragged horizon?

This foothill country is mostly inhabited by Rai and Limbu, their neat thatched houses with ochre and white walls providing the human dimension, while hillside after hillside has been immaculately terraced with crops of rice, millet or sweetcorn. Bananas, oranges and large meaty grapefruit hang from village trees, and in the

61

autumn bougainvillaea and poinsettia add their brilliant colours to an already extravagantly colourful landscape.

Once the trek has dropped to the Tamur River villages become more scarce and the vegetation changes from being predominantly agricultural to that approaching tropical jungle. The route sticks close to the river, frequently climbing and descending as it does, and with no high mountain views to savour until you've left the Tamur behind to climb into the tributary valley of the Ghunsa Khola.

For at least two days the trek battles a way through the uncompromising lower reaches of this narrow, steep-walled valley. As in so many Himalayan regions the high mountains are invariably defended by such gorge-like valleys, a transition zone that is neither foothill nor big mountain in appearance, but which has character all its own with slender waterfalls draining unseen heights and only occasional snippets of snowpeak in view. The valley of the Ghunsa Khola is no exception, and the demands of the trail are quite tough - especially on the steep ascent from Sokathum to Amjilassa.

Midway between the Bhotiya settlements of Phole and Ghunsa one senses that big mountains are not so far away, but you have to trek beyond Ghunsa - almost as far as Khambachen, the last inhabited village - before the full dramatic glory of the major Himalayan peaks is revealed. The first of real stature is Jannu (Kumbhakarna), an amazing piece of mountain architecture flanked by graceful ice-fluted neighbours. Continuing beyond Khambachen the valley makes a long sweeping curve to the north-east then east, passing below the huge iced wall of Kangbachen, followed by Chang Himal (Wedge Peak) before at last you are able to gaze directly onto the Northwest Face of Kangchenjunga itself.

*   *   *

Note that all members of the trek crew, including porters, must be equipped with warm clothing and blankets to deal with the below-freezing night-time temperatures that must be expected in the higher regions of this trek. All food and cooking fuel should also be brought into the area, as the countryside produces sufficient only to meet the needs of the local population.

*   *   *

Two routes are described for the first part of the trek to Dobhan on the Tamur. The first, from the roadhead at Basantpur, is the most heavily used of the longer approaches, and is set out in three day stages (plus a description of the journey from Kathmandu to Basantpur), following the pattern adopted on my most recent trek there. However, unlike the established trekking routes of Annapurna, Khumbu etc, there is not yet a regularly defined pattern of stages - so local porters from Basantpur will almost certainly try to influence shorter days than those described in the following pages. With more and more teahouses and basic lodges being set up throughout the route to Kangchenjunga, and with increased opportunities for camping, it will surely become easier in future to vary the stages to suit each group's timetable.

The second approach trek leading to Dobhan begins at the STOL airstrip at Tumlingtar, and is based on the route of my first Kangchenjunga trek when I walked across this enchanting foothill country in the opposite direction from the big mountains, in order to return to Kathmandu from Tumlingtar itself. A general description of this route only is given, as precise details and timings are not available.

✳ ✳ ✳

KATHMANDU TO BASANTPUR AND
THE TREK TO DOBHAN

The most direct way to reach the start of the trek at Basantpur is to take a morning flight from Kathmandu to Biratnagar, Nepal's second-largest city located just north of the Indian border in the eastern Terai, and arrange for a bus to ferry you from there to the roadhead. In this way it should be possible to get to Basantpur on the same day you leave Kathmandu, thereby being able to start trekking the following morning.

The other method of reaching Basantpur from Kathmandu is via bus all the way. It is a long, but not uninteresting, drive that will take between one and a half and two days - depending how often the vehicle breaks down. My first trip took 26 hours, travelling almost non-stop through one night and the following day. The second trip was better organised, and the journey took two less-frenetic days with an overnight spent in a grotty 'hotel' in an insignificant township in the Terai.

KATHMANDU TO BASANTPUR

From Kathmandu there are just two road routes leading into the Terai, both of which initially head west - in the opposite direction to Kangchenjunga. The Tribhuvan Rajpath is Kathmandu's original vehicular link with India, while the other route is that which breaks away from the Prithvi Rajmarg (Prithvi Highway) at Mugling. The first is a narrow, hair-raising, switchback route, notorious for its blind corners and potential for disaster, and is one that bus drivers not surprisingly prefer to avoid. The alternative adds both time and distance to the journey, but is favoured by anyone with a nervous disposition. In all it's about 600 kilometres (370 miles) to Basantpur by this route.

MUGLING is located 110 kilometres (68 miles) west of Kathmandu, roughly midway between the capital and Pokhara. It's a heaving township of transport cafés and seedy hotels and is where all buses stop for a lunch of *daal bhaat*. The morning's ride to get there from Kathmandu is not without interest, for the road crosses a shallow dip in the valley rim (views to the Ganesh and Manaslu Himals, and a hint of the distant Annapurna range) then twists down to a low-lying valley soon joined by the Trisuli River.

At Mugling the road forks. The continuing Prithvi Highway crosses the Trisuli and hugs the foothills on its way to Pokhara, while the Terai road cuts south through a gorge watered by the Trisuli as far as **NARAYANGADH** where it forks again. Now heading south-east the Mahendra Highway parallels the **CHITWAN NATIONAL PARK** almost as far as **HETAUDA**, a staging post on the Kathmandu-India road at the junction of the Mahendra Highway and Tribhuvan Rajpath.

Joining the Rajpath the journey now travels south across the low Chure Hills and alongside the **PARSA WILDLIFE RESERVE**. The entrance to this is situated just north of **PHATLAYA** where the Mahendra Highway leaves the Rajpath and breaks away to the east, back on course once more for Dharan and Basantpur. The Terai here is punctuated by broad river beds that, once the effects of the

On the way to Ghunsa the trail winds through larch woods.
(Trek 1, Section 3)

Jannu, or Kumbhukarna, looks most impressive when seen from the
approach to Khambachen (Trek 1, Section 3)
The Kangchenjunga Glacier fills the upper valley (Trek 1, Section 3)

monsoon have settled, are almost waterless, a succession of glaring white channels of sand and stone. There are few towns of substance, but numerous small villages are set beside the road with groups of thatched houses and tiny shops on stilts, and you travel through a landscape ploughed by oxen, with scenes of children perched on the dusty backs of water buffalo and, in the orange light of early morning, women striding along misted dykes carrying water in rimmed copper pots.

Beyond the turnoff to Janakpur, perhaps the most fascinating township in the Terai, the road trundles on across flat, almost featureless, agricultural land before reaching the **SAPTA KOSHI**, an incredibly wide river crossed on a pontoon-like bridge that consists of a series of flood-control barriers. Looking off to the right you can see into India a short distance away where the river fans out again.

On the far side of the river the Mahendra Highway curves north and runs alongside the route of a defunct railway, with the **KOSHI TAPPU WILDLIFE RESERVE** spreading north of the Koshi Barrage. In the autumn wigwams of drying reeds are seen in the marshlands, and tall, almost black-skinned men pole their way through the shallows on long dugout canoes or punts laden with harvested reeds. Egrets stalk the same shallows that are bright with the delicate mauve-flowered water hyacinth.

On reaching the crossroads at **ITAHARI** (23km north of Biratnagar) the route turns north and soon brings you to **DHARAN**, an important bazaar town and one-time Gurkha Army Camp, that in 1988 was hit by a powerful earthquake which killed 700 people and flattened most of the buildings. Out of town the road now starts to wind its way into the hills, crosses a ridge at **BHEDETAR** (1420m: 4659ft), then swoops down to the Tamur at **MULGHAT** (280m: 919ft) before climbing over more foothill crests to gain the sturdy-walled township of **DHANKUTA**, the administrative headquarters for Eastern Nepal. Dhankuta is strung along a ridge, but the continuing road bypasses the main township and in another 10 kilometres (6 miles) arrives in **HILE** (1850m: 6070ft) - the end of the paved road in 1997. Hile, which is populated by Rai, Newar and Bhotiya people from the high country further north, is another bazaar town, and on Thursdays the main street is packed with merchants, porters and visitors from the outlying hills.

The final drive of an hour or so bumps from one side of a ridge to the other, and provides tantalising views of Makalu and a whole string of Himalayan giants stretching far off to the west. Just before reaching Basantpur the dirt road comes down a slope on the right-hand side of the wooded crest and, immediately before a final hairpin leading into the town, passes a good flat meadow below the road which makes a fine campsite.

BASANTPUR (2310m: 7579ft) is a grubby, typical roadhead town without obvious appeal. It has a number of shops and lodges, and a police check-post at its southern entrance. Others who have written about it comment on its view of the entire Kangchenjunga massif, which would no doubt improve one's impression of the town, but on both my visits such views were absent, thanks to low cloud or mist.

* * *

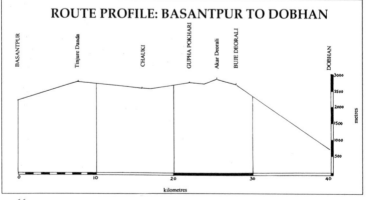

ROUTE PROFILE: BASANTPUR TO DOBHAN

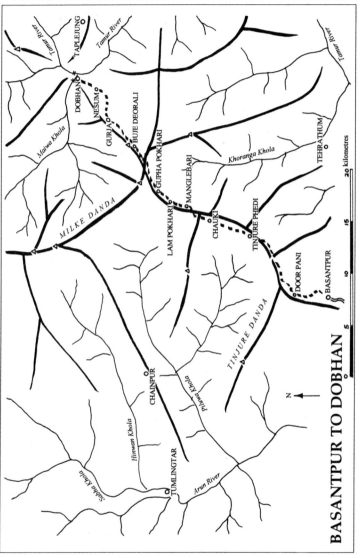

BASANTPUR TO DOBHAN

BASANTPUR - DOOR PANI - CHAUKI

Distance:	16 kilometres (10 miles)
Time:	3¹/₂-4 hours
Start altitude:	2310 metres (7579ft)
High point:	Tinjure Danda (2900m: 9514ft)
Height gain:	590 metres (1936ft)
Height loss:	240 metres (787ft)

This first stage of the trek is not too demanding, for it makes a long and steady climb to the wooded Tinjure Danda on an easy trail, passing through a few minor settlements with very little sign of cultivation - quite unlike the countryside visited in a couple of days' time, and in direct contrast to the northern side of this range of hills where, overlooking the Arun Valley, terraces fill every view. Part of today's walk follows a traditional trade route linking Chainpur in the Arun Valley with the Tamur, and in the next couple of days you will come across several other paths traversing the Tinjure and Milke Dandas that have been in use by laden porters for who knows how many generations. This crest of the Tinjure Danda, midway between Door Pani and Chauki, is clothed in rhododendron forest, but the final section of the walk crosses open pastures below the ridge where stupendous views of Makalu and the Khumbu Himal are unforgettable.

* * *

In the centre of Basantpur the main street forks by a water supply. Take the left-hand option, which is more narrow than the other, leading between teahouses, lodges and shops. It soon climbs above the village onto a broad and open ridge where the trail makes several braidings, passes a few solitary houses and, 20 minutes from the start, comes onto the dirt road again. Five minutes later leave the road by taking a path rising between houses.

The dirt road snakes its way along the hillside and makes for the Tinjure Danda. It would be perfectly feasible to remain on the road as far as Door Pani, but the old trail is much better, and although at times it is necessary to use the road, most of the time the trail avoids it. After about 45 minutes come to the small village of **TUDE DEORALI** (2460m: 8071ft) where the road forks. The left branch is the route to Chainpur, but we bear right, then take a path rising past the upper houses of the village and continue on through woodland.

In a little over half an hour after leaving Tude Deorali you come to a group of simple teahouses. This is **DOOR PANI** (2680m: 8793ft 1hr 20mins *refreshments - possible camping if you started late from Basantpur*). Continue uphill, and in just under 2 hours you will top the ridge at 2860m (9383ft) among rhododendrons. The trail then winds along the crest with views between the trees into valley systems to left and right, and comes to another group of teahouses perched on the crest at **PANCH POKHARI** (2850m: 9350ft 2hrs 10mins *refreshments*).

About 15 minutes later the trail crosses to the left side of the ridge crest at 2900m (9514ft) and makes a long slanting descent through dank, mossy, rhododendron forest leading to **TINJURE PHEDI** (2hrs 50mins *refreshments*), where there are more simple teahouses gathered beside the trail. Beyond these the way soon leads over pleasant open grassland with views growing in extent to include Makalu[1], Lhotse Shar[2], Everest[3] (just) and the long flat-looking ridge of Chamlang[4] - a wonderful sight. Across this pasture you come to **CHAUKI**.

CHAUKI (2660m: 8727ft 3hrs 35mins *accommodation, refreshments*) consists of a few houses grouped either side of a paved street, down the centre of which is a long *chautaara* on which porters rest their loads. The village boasts one or two simple lodges, shops and teahouses. There is a police check-post and, off to the left, the village school, with plenty of space for camping in the open pastures.

Points of Interest Along the Way:
1: MAKALU (8481m: 27,825ft) is the world's fifth highest mountain. Although it was photographed from the north and north-west as early as 1921 by members of the Everest reconnaissance, and from the air in 1933, the first attempt to climb the mountain was not made until 1954 when members of an American expedition reached a high point of about 7150 metres. In the autumn of that year a French reconnaissance expedition, led by Lucien Devies, reached 7800 metres. The following year Devies organised a follow-up expedition with Jean Franco as leader. On 15 May 1955 the summit was gained

by Couzy and Terray. Two further ascents were made by other members of the expedition on 16 and 17 May. (See *Makalu* by Jean Franco, Cape, 1957.) Makalu, and the country south and west of it, was made part of the Makalu-Barun National Park in 1992. Its boundaries spread from the depths of the Arun Valley westward to the edge of the Everest (Sagarmatha) National Park.

2: LHOTSE SHAR (8398m: 27,552ft). Lhotse is the principal summit in a long ridge of mountains to the south of Mount Everest. The alignment of this ridge is west-east, and with Lhotse Shar being Lhotse's closest neighbour, it is this peak which actually blocks the higher summit from view when seen on the approach to Chauki. Lhotse Shar was first climbed by S. Mayerl and R. Walter of an Austrian expedition in May 1970, their route of ascent being via the south-east ridge.

3: MOUNT EVEREST (8848m: 29,028ft) is, of course, the world's highest mountain. Known also as Sagarmatha and Chomolungma, it straddles the border between Nepal and Tibet. All pre-war attempts to climb it were made from the north, but with the 'closing' of Tibet coinciding with the 'opening' of Nepal after the war, Everest was finally won by Hillary and Tenzing on the British expedition led by John Hunt in 1953. The story of Everest is well-known, the bibliography being perhaps the largest devoted to any of the world's mountains. But see *Everest* by Walt Unsworth (Oxford Illustrated Press/Grafton Books, 1989) for the definitive version.

4: CHAMLANG (7319m: 24,012ft). This impressive-looking mountain has an 8km long ridge which never falls below 7000 metres between its two main summits. An expedition from the New Zealand Alpine Club explored the south-eastern side in 1954, but the first ascent was achieved in 1962 by members of the Hokkaido University's expedition approaching via the Hongu Khola.

* * *

CHAUKI - GUPHA POKHARI - BUJE DEORALI

Distance:	12 kilometres (7¹/₂ miles)
Time:	5 hours
Start altitude:	2660 metres (8727ft)

High point:	Akar Deorali (2950m: 9678ft)
Height gain:	365 metres (1198ft)
Height loss:	205 metres (673ft)

This is a splendid day's trekking on good trails and with Himalayan snowpeaks forming a broad panorama for much of the way. The route passes through a few small villages and groups of temporary shelters provided for porters on the trade route to Taplejung; it crosses open meadows, and twists among rhododendron forests. Some trekking groups go no further than Gupha Pokhari on this stage, and any local porters with you will no doubt try to insist that this is the only place to camp. Certainly there are few options for overnighting beyond Gupha Pokhari, other than at Buje Deorali, until you begin the descent to Dobhan, that is, but to stop at Gupha makes for a very short day if you only began at Chauki. But whatever the length of stage is chosen by your Sirdar, hopefully you'll have those stimulating views to enjoy.

* * *

Leaving Chauki the trail continues across broad pastures with Makalu dominating views ahead until the way enters a section crowded with shrubs and trees, but about 25 minutes after setting out you turn a corner and gain a sudden magnificent view of the Kangchenjunga[1] massif with shapely Jannu[2] just to the left of the main block of mountains. A few minutes after this the trail comes to a more open hillside from where Makalu and the Khumbu Himal once more appear to the north-west. At this point you have four 8000 metre peaks in view, while off to the right the long Singalila Ridge forms the Nepalese-Indian border.

About 40 minutes from Chauki you come to the cluster of houses of **MANGLEBARI** (2620m: 8596ft *refreshments - possible camping below in a hillside scoop near a small lake*). The village boasts a simple porters' lodge and a few shops. The trail forks. Continue ahead (the right-hand trail) rising a little, then cutting across the flank of hillside on a gentle contour with Kangchenjunga seen directly ahead, but about 80 kilometres (50 miles) away. The hillside is patched with groves of rhododendron whose pink bark is hung about with tatters of lichen, mosses, ferns and, in places, with tree orchids.

The path meanders through these rhododendron woods and comes to a string of temporary teahouses with woven bamboo roofs (1hr 35mins *refreshments*). Half an hour later you cross the ridge at 2905m (9531ft), then cut along the left-hand side to reach **LAM POKHARI**, a few houses built beside two small lakes. Note the memorial stones fitted into a *chautaara* here. Beyond this tiny settlement the trail continues along the crest of the ridge before sloping down to the village of **GUPHA POKHARI** (2870m: 9416ft 3hrs 10mins *accommodation, refreshments - possible camping*).

The village, which has been settled by people of Tibetan stock, straddles a paved street with a long *chautaara* down the centre. There are several shops and a few lodges, a Buddhist shrine, prayer flags and another collection of memorial stones. The lake, or tarn, from which Gupha takes its name (*pokhari* means lake) is found in the grassland left of the village. Needless to say, the water is polluted. There's another path junction on the edge of the village, and just beyond it a shop or two and a teahouse. The left-hand trail skirts the flank of the Milke Danda to link with the old trade route from Chainpur to Dobhan and Taplejung, while yours is the alternative option.

Losing views of Makalu now, follow the continuing path which goes up the ridge ahead for a short distance before slanting off along the right-hand slope. A steady descending traverse is then made towards an obvious wooded saddle ahead, followed by a short climb that takes you to that saddle at 2870m (9416ft). This is reached about 4 hours after leaving Chauki. Instead of crossing this saddle the path continues directly up the ridge to gain a 'pass' marked by a few prayer flags on bamboo wands. This is known as **AKAR DEORALI** (2950m: 9678ft 4hrs 10mins).

The trail now descends among more rhododendrons. It's a corrugated route with lots of ups and downs and limited views, thanks to the crowded vegetation. Then, about 40 minutes from Akar Deorali, you come to the group of basic timber and bamboo houses of **BUJE DEORALI** (2820m: 9252ft 4hrs 50mins). Behind the right-hand building is a small grass meadow with space for a few tents. From the lip of the banking ridge one gains a stunning view of Kangchenjunga - sunset and sunrise views are especially fine.

Points of Interest Along the Way:

1: KANGCHENJUNGA (8586m: 28,169ft) is the world's third highest mountain, and was climbed for the first time on 25 May 1955 by George Band and Joe Brown of a British expedition led by Charles Evans. The following day the summit was reached by Norman Hardie and Tony Streather. A brief history of the mountain is given in Appendix A, but see *Kangchenjunga: the Untrodden Peak* by Charles Evans (Hodder & Stoughton, 1956) for an account of the first ascent.

2: JANNU (7710m: 25,295ft) was renamed Kumbhakarna by the Nepalese. It is the most distinctive of Kangchenjunga's satellites, with an impressive chisel-shaped summit supported by two ridges resembling 'the back of a huge chair'. In 1957 it was visited by Guido Magnone and two companions who studied the peak from three different sides, each of which seemed well protected either by ice-plastered ridges or by steep, and in some cases overhanging, rock walls. Two years later Magnone returned with a team led by Jean Franco, and after their chosen route above the Yamatari Glacier was hit by an avalanche soon after arrival, they turned their attention to the south-east ridge, reaching 7425 metres before being turned back. In 1962 Franco was back with Lionel Terray to lead a successful French expedition which managed to place all the climbers on the summit in two successive days. (See *At Grips With Jannu* by Jean Franco & Lionel Terray, Gollancz, 1967.)

* * *

BUJE DEORALI - GURJA - DOBHAN

Distance:	12 kilometres (7¹/₂ miles)
Time:	5 hours
Start altitude:	2820 metres (9252ft)
Low point:	Dobhan (760m: 2493ft)
Height loss:	2060 metres (6759ft)

Downhill almost all the way, this is the finest stage of the trek so far. Below the initial forests of rhododendron, hazel and chestnut trees, attractive villages nestle in a landscape of warm colours. With the valley of the Tamur far below, terraced hillsides gaze off to Kangchenjunga, and the trail goes down among rice paddies and fields of millet, passing family-sized banana plantations, orange trees and through avenues of poinsettia. According to the map, the horizontal distance travelled on this stage is slight, but with so much height to lose in order to reach the Tamur's banks below Dobhan, it will seem much longer.

* * *

From Buje Deorali the path, which is rough in places, descends through rhododendron forest broken here and there to allow teasing mountain views across the depths of the Tamur Valley to the distant Himalaya. (Note the tree orchids that adorn a number of mossy-trunked trees, as well as straggling cords of clematis hanging over the trail.) After 30 minutes you emerge from the forest for a moment by a simple teahouse (2540m: 8333ft) and a *chautaara* from which a truly magnificent view is had of Kangchenjunga and Jannu; enough to stop you in your tracks.

The trail re-enters forest, goes through more clearings and eventually comes out below the wooded upper slopes to yet more stunning views. Across the Tamur's valley the ridgetop airstrip of Taplejung (Suketar) can just be seen, as can the clustered houses of Taplejung itself some way below. But it is the mighty wall of snowpeaks that commands attention, and it is from here that you can make out the two main valley systems that form calipers round the Kangchenjunga massif. It is tempting to speculate on the route to be followed in the days and weeks ahead. Fifteen minutes later you come to the first houses of **GURJA** (2165m: 7103ft 1hr 35mins).

In the spring of 1979 Joe Tasker came along this trail on his way to the Northwest Face of Kangchenjunga with Peter Boardman, Doug Scott and Georges Bettembourg:

"For two days we walked along the crest of a rounded ridge dividing the Arun and Tamur valleys... We reached a village at the end of the ridge and from there we had to descend to the valley, to the jungle and heat once again. Above the village, in the sky hovering white and unobtrusive in the distance so I thought it was a cloud, was the mountain. We were not yet halfway there and it stood up big and massive... Suddenly I was aware of how small we were."

(Joe Tasker: *Savaga Arena*)

Wandering down through the scattered village of Gurja you pass neat thatched houses adorned with marigold garlands, and in the autumn with cobs of sweetcorn hanging beneath the eaves, and racks of corn drying on stilts nearby. In the lower part of the village there's a lodge and a couple of simple shops.

Continuing downhill the trail edges numerous terraced fields, then into a belt of bamboo followed by chir pine. About three hours after setting out you descend alongside the school at **NESUM** (1470m: 4823ft) and reach the village ten minutes later. Like Gurja, Nesum is also a scattered village, its houses dotted about the terraces.

BHAJOGARA (970m: 3182ft 4hrs 10mins) is the next village. More compact than its higher neighbours, the houses are gathered on a short spur projecting to the side of a large pipal tree. The main trail descends to the left of the village and, passing more terraced fields of rice and millet, reaches another school about 25 minutes later. So come to the first houses of **DOBHAN** (760m: 2493ft 4hrs 40mins *accommodation, refreshments - camping possible below the town*).

DOBHAN[1] is an important but untidy bazaar, the largest on this route since leaving Basantpur. It has a police check-post, shops, bank, teahouses and a lodge or two. Electricity poles and sagging cables hint at technology. There is also a telephone facility. The population of Dobhan is mixed; many are Newaris, but Tibetans have also settled here. A good campsite is to be found on the north bank of the Maiwa Khola, and there is another at the confluence of this river with the Tamur. The way to both of these is along the continuing route, as follows.

At the police post bear left to pass several shops, and you will shortly come to a suspension bridge over the Maiwa Khola. On the far side of this there are many more shops. (The first camping area is off to the left, on the river's left bank.) Continue along the street between shops, heading for a second suspension bridge which spans the Tamur. Shortly before reaching it, however, cut off to the right on a pathway through a few small fields, then down a slope to a secluded meadow bordered by trees on a spit of land between the two rivers.

Points of Interest Along the Way:

1: DOBHAN In November 1848 plant hunter Joseph Hooker arrived here on his first journey of exploration that was to take him close to the base of Kangchenjunga. In the classic account of his travels, *Himalayan Journals*, he refers to Dobhan as Mywa Guola. This is how he describes it:

"Mywa Guola (or bazaar) is a large village frequented by Nepalese and Tibetans, who bring salt, wool, gold, musk, and blankets, to exchange for rice, coral, and other commodities; and a custom-house officer is stationed there, with a few soldiers. The houses are of wood, and well built: the public ones are large, with verandahs, and galleries of carved wood; the workmanship is of Chinese character, and inferior to that of Katmandoo; but in the same style, and unlike anything I had previously seen."

* * *

The continuing trek to Pangpema resumes on page 84.

* * *

TUMLINGTAR TO DOBHAN

An alternative to using Biratnagar as a start to the trek is to book a flight from Kathmandu to Tumlingtar on the Arun, and trek from there via Chainpur to join the main route described either at Gupha Pokhari, or at

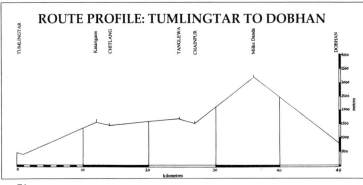

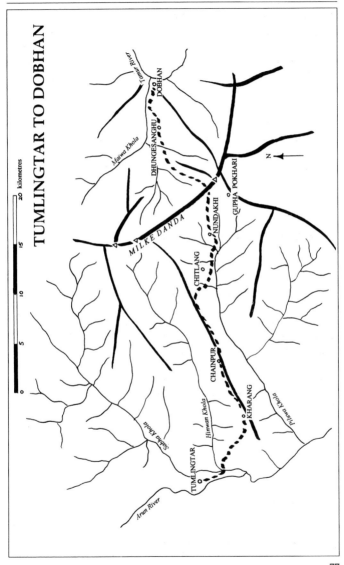

TUMLINGTAR TO DOBHAN

Dobhan on the banks of the Tamur River. One problem with this, however, is the need to arrange local porters in advance. Another is the cost of transporting food and equipment by air. Some trekking agents send this by road to Hile (or Basantpur) in the care of the kitchen crew and a few sherpas, from where porters can be hired. They then trek across country to meet the Sirdar and group members at either the Tumlingtar airstrip, or at Chainpur.

* * *

TUMLINGTAR - CHAINPUR

Distance:	14 kilometres (8½ miles)
Time:	4½-5 hours
Start altitude:	457 metres (1499ft)
High point:	Katarigaon (1335m: 4380ft)
Height gain:	878 metres (2881ft)

For a first day's walk the trek up to Chainpur is pretty demanding, for there is a fair amount of height to be gained, and this is, after all, low, humid country. In both the spring and autumn trekking seasons, this is likely to be a sticky walk. Much will depend on your time of arrival at Tumlingtar whether you reach Chainpur or not, but you should in any case allow a full day for this stage.

* * *

From the broad meadowland airstrip a good path heads south between fields, and after about 15 minutes, just beyond a group of houses and shops, you bear left (the continuing trail is the one which goes to Hile) and descend to the valley of the Sabha Khola at its confluence with the Hinwan Khola tributary. Some maps indicate a bridge south of this point. When I was there one supposedly had a choice of either taking a ferry (which was not in evidence) or wading the river. We waded.

Having gained the left bank of the Hinwan Khola, take the path which starts to climb the eastern hillside. It becomes quite steep for a while as you rise among sugar cane, bananas, rice and millet, the soil almost red when it has been turned by the plough. As you gain height so hinted views reveal snowpeaks of the Khumbu Himal to the north-west, while below, the valley of the Arun[1] makes a broad swathe between rolling foothills. About 2 hours from Tumlingtar you come onto a ridge crest at a teahouse, and from there the way continues up to **KHARANG**, reached about 50 minutes later. This village has a paved street lined with neat shops, and from there the trail is likely to be busy with locals.

Along the ridge to Chainpur views open to show more of the long Himalayan horizon, of which Makalu and Chamlang are of particular note. You pass through bamboo thickets, and between trees, shrubs and spindly poinsettias, gaze down on a vast array of terraces and pass a Hindu temple at **KATARIGAON**. The trail is a broad one, and a little under an hour and a half from Kharang it brings you into **CHAINPUR**[2] (1315m: 4314ft 4hrs 30mins *accommodation, refreshments, camping*), a prosperous white-painted township set in a saddle of the hills. Permits will need to be checked at the police post.

Points of Interest Along the Way:

1: THE ARUN RIVER drains out of the Himalaya east of Makalu, and is one of the most important of all rivers in Eastern Nepal. For a number of years a highly controversial $700 million hydro project, known as Arun III, was planned to be built with money from the World Bank and other international finance agencies. The scheme was met with fierce opposition, not only from the environmental lobby, and at the time of writing the plan is believed to have been shelved.

2: CHAINPUR is noted for its brassware. The Newaris who moved here from Kathmandu and joined the traditional Rai hill-folk of the district, have established a thriving brass industry in the town. Their workshops line the busy paved street, and it's possible to see casting work in progress, the furnaces built just behind shop fronts, and the sound of tapping coming, it seems, from every building. The town has many shops, teahouses and lodges, a post office, schools and temples. There are houses with carved wooden balconies, and gardens bright with orange trees and bananas and lush bougainvillaea. When camping overnight, sunset and sunrise views over the distant Himalaya are magical.

* * *

CHAINPUR - CHITLANG

Distance:	13 kilometres (8 miles)
Time:	3¹/₂-4 hours
Start altitude:	1315 metres (4314ft)
High point:	Tanglewa (1570m: 5151ft)
Height gain:	255 metres (837ft)

This stage of the trek is less demanding than yesterday's, for although there are ups and downs (as always in Nepal), these are mostly gentle. It's a well-cultivated region, with terraces of rice and millet, and houses dotted along the route - trim thatch over white and ochre painted walls. Several teahouses are passed; there are small villages and big views, and several streams to cross on log bridges or stepping stones.

* * *

From Chainpur a well-used trail heads east into the valley of the Piluwa Khola and then makes a cross-country route to Chauki, which is met at the end of the first stage of the main trek described above. For the route to Chitlang, however, walk up the paved trail which climbs above the town. After passing some houses the way leads among trees, while both sides of the ridge are stepped with terraced fields. A little over an hour after setting out you arrive in the ridge-top village of **POKHARI** (Sita Pokhari; 1515m: 4970ft) whose large school, built in 1957, caters for 450 children from the surrounding countryside. There are several small shops in the village, and a good view of Chamlang and the summit cone of Makalu.

The trail continues above **MAYAM**, rises again then follows a regular contour way above the valley of the Piluwa Khola, with terraces everywhere. The day's high point is reached at a teahouse in the small settlement of **TANGLEWA** (1570m: 5151ft 2hrs 10mins *refreshments*).

As the way progresses you pass numerous houses dotted along the hillside, and there will probably be plenty of activity in the terraces and along the trail. Streams are crossed and the strung-out village of **CHITLANG** is visited on the way down to a stream which is crossed on stepping stones, followed by a suspension bridge over the Piluwa Khola (1360m: 4462ft 3hrs 40mins). Camping is possible on terraces nearby when the harvest has been taken.

* * *

CHITLANG - MILKE DANDA

Distance:	9 kilometres (5¹/₂ miles)
Time:	5-5¹/₂ hours
Start altitude:	1360 metres (4462ft)
High point:	Milke Danda (c.3100m: 10,170ft)
Height gain:	1740 metres (5709ft)
Height loss:	600 metres (1969ft)

Between the valleys of the Piluwa Khola and the Maiwa Khola (which feeds into the Tamur at Dobhan) runs the long wooded ridge of the Milke Danda, trending from north-west to south-east. Crossing this ridge is the major obstacle on the route. It's not a difficult crossing, of course, but since the Milke Danda maintains an altitude of around 3000 metres (9800ft), there is a fair amount of height to gain when starting from the Piluwa Khola. On this stage there's also an opportunity to cut across to Gupha Pokhari and there join the main Basantpur to Dobhan route, if that is the plan.

* * *

The valley of the Piluwa Khola is a tight wedge, and the climb out of it is quite steep at first, twisting between drystone walls or terraced banks, with numerous houses set in a prosperous landscape. **NUNDHAKI** is a large Rai and Limbu village stepped up the hillside. Set upon a sunny slope the first part is reached about half an hour from the river, but it will take another half-hour or more before you've passed all the way through. Note the coffin-like gravestones beside the trail.

In a meadow near the village school (*possible camping*) the trail divides. The right-hand option heads up and along the slopes of the Milke Danda to reach Gupha Pokhari in about 3-3¹/₂ hours from Nundhaki. At Gupha Pokhari you can join the main Basantpur-Dobhan trail described above.

From Nundhaki school continue on the left-hand path as it maintains a steep climb towards the Milke Danda ridge. This winding trail can be greasy after rain, and it leads eventually onto the tree-crowned crest at around 3100 metres. Wandering along the ridge, sometimes on the right-hand slope, sometimes on the left, you cross open meadows with a couple of stone huts where you may see yaks or *dzopkyos* (male yak and cow crossbreeds) grazing. With clear visibility, Kangchenjunga and Jannu should be in view from here. (On my crossing clouds hid all but the topmost portion of Jannu.)

From a saddle in the ridge the trail begins to descend. Mostly at an easy gradient the way takes you through forest, losing about 600m (1969ft) before coming to an undulating meadow in a clearing on the eastern side of the Milke Danda. This makes a good campsite, altitude about 2500 metres (8202ft).

* * *

MILKE DANDA - DOBHAN

Distance:	13 kilometres (8 miles)
Time:	4-4¹/₂ hours
Start altitude:	2500 metres (8202ft)
Low point:	Dobhan (760m: 2493ft)
Height loss:	1740 metres (5709ft)

On this descent to Dobhan the route returns to lush terracing and villages once more, with views to the Kangchenjunga massif teasing far ahead - which all makes for a very pleasant day's trekking.

* * *

For a while the descent goes through woodland, then out to an open hillside where the trail forks. Both paths eventually lead to Dhungesanghu. The left-hand option is the one described. This soon leads into cultivated fields as you continue down to the busy village of **SANGHU** where there is a large school and a shop. Winding round the edge of numerous terraces the trail, which is mostly a good one, broad and well trodden, makes a traverse here,

Typical house near Dhungesanghu

descent there - nearly always with glorious unhindered views to Kangchenjunga and its lofty neighbours on the skyline. Eventually you come to a minor stream which is a tributary of the Maiwa Khola, and pass a watermill.

Going through a tree-clad section the path continues among terraces, now on a helter-skelter course, until you reach **DHUNGESANGHU** (c.1400m: 4593ft), a village of corrugated-iron roofs whose houses cover a wide area. There's at least one shop, and a school some way below. On the way to the school you pass a water cistern with crumbling gargoyles and bamboo pipes. *(Camping is possible on terraces between the main village and the school, if required.)*

Below the school the descent is maintained among more terraces, through avenues of trees and poinsettias above the valley of the Maiwa Khola, and at last you enter **DOBHAN** (760m: 2493ft 4-4¹/₂ hours *accommodation, refreshments, camping*), a busy bazaar at the confluence of the Maiwa Khola and Tamur River. This important township has a police check-post, a number of shops, a bank, telephone and a simple lodge or two. There are two possible campsites: the first is located on the left bank of the Maiwa Khola

83

and is reached by crossing the first suspension bridge then turning left; the other is gained just before reaching the second suspension bridge (which crosses the Tamur), where you take a narrow path off to the right. This leads through small fields, then down a slope to a spit of land between the two rivers.

* * *

DOBHAN TO PANGPEMA

The two initial foothill routes having now combined at Dobhan, the continuing trek to the Kangchenjunga North Base Camp at Pangpema is described in the following stages.

* * *

DOBHAN - MITLUNG

Distance:	12 kilometres (7¹/₂ miles)
Time:	3¹/₂-4 hours
Start altitude:	760 metres (2493ft)
High point:	Mitlung (995m: 3264ft)
Height gain:	235 metres (771ft)

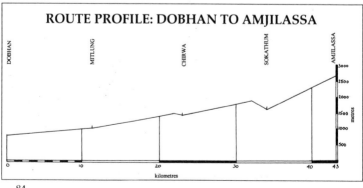

ROUTE PROFILE: DOBHAN TO AMJILASSA

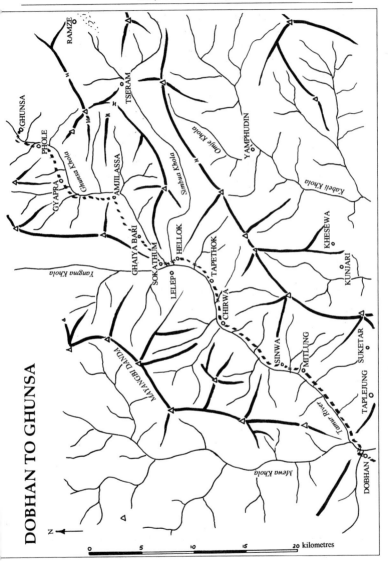

DOBHAN TO GHUNSA

N ←

0   5   10   15   20 kilometres

Three days after leaving the roadhead the trek now enters its second phase. The next three days will be spent beside the roaring Tamur River heading roughly north-east on undulating trails and through jungle-like forests with little habitation in sight. Where villages do exist, these are mostly perched high above the river. Sections of the route are subjected to occasional monsoon-induced landslip, and several tributary streams are crossed on makeshift bridges. It all makes for an interesting trek. There has been no long-established trade route through this part of the Tamur Valley, so trails are often poor, and the few teahouse facilities that are encountered are mostly due to the influx of foreign trekking and mountaineering groups. Even so, they are neither as numerous nor as well stocked as the teahouses in the Annapurna, Khumbu or Langtang regions. Gone now are the big Himalayan views, for the steep walls of the valley effectively block out any sign of the snowpeaks with which you've grown familiar over the past few days. Nonetheless there is still plenty to enjoy.

This first stage along the Tamur, though not far in linear distance, is fairly tough and, thanks to the rough trail and increased temperatures, can be quite difficult for heavily-laden porters. There will no doubt be plenty of excuses to rest before you get to Mitlung.

* * *

There are trails on both banks of the Tamur[1], although some maps fail to show that which follows the east (left) bank - the route described here. Cross the Tamur River on the big suspension bridge, but do not climb the steps on the far side. (This is the route to Taplejung taken by groups heading for the south side of Kangchenjunga.) Instead, immediately across the bridge bear left on a narrow, indistinct trail which cuts along the edge of a series of fields. Within the first half-hour after setting out the way climbs a little, opposite the confluence of the Mewa Khola and Tamur River, beyond which the valley curves to the right and becomes somewhat wider. The path then descends to river-level.

About 40 minutes from Dobhan a small village (Handrung?) can be seen on the opposite side of the Tamur, partially screened by a long bank of bougainvillaea - a blaze of colour in October/November. The east bank trail is narrow all the way. Sometimes it eases through sandy beds between rocks and boulders smoothed by the river when in spate; sometimes it cuts over rough meadows with streams

Delicate bridge crossing in the Tamur Valley

running across; sometimes alongside sub-tropical forest, and at other times it squeezes among jungle-like growth. A dry river bed is crossed by the mouth of a tributary glen, then the way climbs to pass through rice terraces high above the river and comes to a lone building at 890m (2920ft 2hrs 5mins). Five minutes later pass another simple building used as a teahouse overlooking a suspension bridge which spans the Tamur and unites the west bank trail with ours. The village of Thumma is on the far side.

The path now descends and forks. Cut right on a continuing trail that makes a contour for a while before resuming its up and down course through more jungley forest. After 3 hours of trekking from Dobhan the way leads into the mouth of a gorge-like tributary whose river is negotiated on a two-pole bridge. Beyond this somewhat delicate crossing there is a sharp pull up the north bank to a small house set beside the trail, and with a cluster of banana trees nearby. In a little over 3½ hours an avenue of frangipani directs the trail into the village of **MITLUNG**.

MITLUNG (995m: 3264ft *refreshments, camping possible*) is a huddled Chhetri village of white and ochre-painted houses, with a

87

teahouse and a few shops, and a small but pleasant camping area on a terrace behind the last group of houses on the left of the trail.

Points of Interest Along the Way:

1: THE TAMUR RIVER After the Arun, the Tamur is the last important river in north-east Nepal. Rising just below the Tiptala Pass north-west of Walungchung Gola (visited by Hooker), it receives all the waters draining from the south and west sides of the Kangchenjunga massif as it flows southward, parallel with the Indian border before uniting with the Arun near Dharan. From its confluence with the Arun, the Tamur becomes known as the Sapta Koshi, that broad waterway crossed by road near the Koshi Tappu Wildlife Reserve mentioned earlier.

* * *

MITLUNG - SINWA - CHIRWA

Distance:	11 kilometres (7 miles)
Time:	4-4½ hours
Start altitude:	995 metres (3264ft)
High point:	1430 metres (4692ft)
Height gain:	435 metres (1427ft)

The trail improves a little on this stage, but the route is still quite demanding with plenty of ups and downs, and with more streams to cross on sometimes questionable bridges. The valley is a sinuous one, broad in places, constricted in others, the river thundering one minute over boulder-choked rapids, then a few minutes later it appears calm and placid where the level eases. In both the spring and autumn trekking seasons the temperature in this valley can be humid, and opportunities for refreshment at the few teahouses along the trail will be welcome.

* * *

Outside Mitlung the improved trail soon ascends a rough stone staircase against a cliff, tops a high steep bluff, then descends immediately to more rice terraces, and a little over half an hour from the start you come to a huddle of woven bamboo houses with thatched roofs set in the mouth of a tributary glen. The Sisne Khola (draining the unseen Pathibhara) is crossed on a suspension bridge of dubious quality at about 1030m (3379ft), and the trail continues thereafter high above the Tamur with good views down onto rice terraces. Most of these are on the west bank where the slopes spill out in steps towards the river.

Come to an attractive collection of thatched houses (1hr 15mins) with bananas, oranges and thickets of bamboo growing around them, and just beyond these the trail forks. Take the left-hand option and slope down the hillside with a suspension bridge seen crossing the Tamur below. Passing between terraces, in a few minutes enter the busy village of **SINWA** (1055m: 3461ft 1hr 25mins *refreshments*). The street here is lined with several shops and teahouses, and at the far end there's a police check-post where permits must be shown.

After leaving Sinwa the way descends to the river bed, the valley at this point being quite broad. Ahead another tributary valley enters from the left, and just beyond this confluence the Tamur Valley narrows and curves to the right, the trail now sneaking along the edge of more jungle-like forest.

This stretch of the valley was described by Hooker:

"...the valley contracts much, and the Tambur [sic] becomes a turbulent river, shooting along its course with immense velocity, torn into foam as it lashes the spurs of rock that flank it, and the enormous boulders with which its bed is strewn. ... In the contracted parts of the valley, the mountains often dip to the river-bed in precipices, under the ledges of which wild bees build pendulous nests, looking like huge bats suspended by their wings; they are two or three feet long, and as broad at the top, whence they taper downwards: the honey is much sought for, except in spring, when it is said to be poisoned by Rhododendron flowers."

(Joseph Dalton Hooker: *Himalayan Journals*)

It is in search of honey from such nests that hunters still risk life and limb by suspending themselves from bamboo ladders - as described and photographed by Eric Valli and Diane Summers in *Honey Hunters of Nepal* (Thames & Hudson, 1988).

About 50 minutes after leaving Sinwa the trail curves into another narrow tributary glen, crosses its stream on a rough bridge of logs

89

and bamboo, then climbs another 60 metres or so, passing a couple of teahouses on the way. In 2hrs 35mins come to a scattering of houses at 1265m (4150ft) - bright with hibiscus and bougainvillaea in October/November. The trail remains high above the river while the valley turns more wild and gorge-like, with only a few sparse patches of cultivation, and several landslides that have to be crossed.

After 3hrs 20mins you will reach another settlement at 1385m (4544ft), and a few minutes later the trail cuts down to cross another stream. Just before reaching the stream a second path breaks off to the right - this route leads to Taplejung, and is one that is sometimes taken by groups aiming for the north side of Kangchenjunga having flown in to the STOL airstrip at Suketar. Continuing, the main trail rises once more, tops a high point of about 1430m (4692ft), then slopes down to **CHIRWA**.

CHIRWA (1330m: 4364ft 4hrs 10mins *accommodation, refreshments, camping*) is a close huddle of thatched houses, a very simple lodge and a couple of shops. Nearby there is a suspension bridge over the Tamur, and 15 minutes beyond the houses a good campsite is located on a broad terrace above the river.

* * *

CHIRWA - TAPETHOK - SOKATHUM

Distance:	11 kilometres (7 miles)
Time:	4 hours
Start altitude:	1330 metres (4364ft)
Highest point:	1735 metres (5692ft)
Height gain:	405 metres (1329ft)

Another fine day's trekking, this stage provides ever-evolving landscapes and a variety of vegetation. There are several fairly steep uphill and downhill sections, some of which are quite exposed, and more interesting bridge crossings. Towards the end of the day you cross the Simbua Khola, whose valley leads to the south side of Kangchenjunga - and finish the trek soon after in the lower reaches of the Ghunsa Khola which drains the Kangchenjunga Glacier flowing from the mountain's north-west face.

* * *

North of Chirwa the trail crosses water-worn rocks bearing evidence that the river once flowed through the valley at a much higher level than it does today, and not long after leaving the campsite you pass a splendid rock wall smoothed and whorled at a bend in the valley where the Tamur formerly pounded against it. Just beyond this the trail forks. A minor path drops to the left into more sub-tropical forest, and offers a shorter option than the main trail - the two reunite about 45 minutes later where the valley opens out. (The lower route is narrow, but interesting, although the upper trail should be easier for laden porters.)

Five minutes after the two paths come together again (50mins from camp), cross a suspension bridge over a major tributary, and in a further 5 minutes there is a collection of eight memorials set beside the trail - oblong stones decorated with images, such as the sun, swastikas (for good luck), tridents and faces. Shortly after these have been passed you come to another suspension bridge, this one spanning the Tamur. Do not cross this, but continue ahead to a few teahouses (1430m: 4692ft 1hour *refreshments*). Just to the right, near the suspension bridge, you'll find a police check-post. Above that stand the houses of **TAPETHOK**.

Once more the valley contracts beyond Tapethok and there is no more cultivation for a while. The trail climbs high above the river before descending again; the Tamur now milky-blue as a sure sign of its glacial origins, and the first sighting of a snowpeak glimpsed far ahead - a conical peak that appears to be blocking the Tamur's gorge.

Two hours from Chirwa cross another suspension bridge, this one over the Thakyak Khola (1530m: 5020ft), on the far side of which stands a solitary house, with a woven bamboo-walled watermill just below. The path climbs again past one or two more houses, then twists steeply up the hillside to gain fine views along the heavily-wooded gorge and into the blue, foam-flecked river far beneath. Having gained a high point of about 1660m (5446ft), the trail then makes a pleasant belvedere with teasing hinted views of snowpeaks ahead. After a while the way descends through woodland, and 2hrs 40mins from Chirwa you pass above yet another suspension bridge spanning the Tamur River. Climbing again the path curves into the mouth of the Simbua Khola's valley near the village of **HELLOK**.

From here the trail descends steeply on a rough stone staircase to a bridge where you cross the Simbua Khola (3hrs 10mins), the river which drains the Yalung Glacier on the south side of Kangchenjunga. A plaque on the north side of the bridge explains that it was built in 1984, and has a span of 54 metres. Turn left to rise steadily above the Tamur again, reaching a high point at 1735m (5692ft) as you turn into the mouth of the Ghunsa Khola Valley and slope down to the last suspension bridge of the day. On the south bank by the bridge stands a solitary house inhabited by Bhotiya people who sometimes have bottled drinks for sale (1670m: 5479ft 3hrs 45mins *refreshments*).

Cross the bridge and bear right away from the Tamur at last. (To reach the village of Sokathum turn left.) Five minutes from the bridge come to a meadowland above the Ghunsa Khola, with a couple of buildings, one of which is a shop (1680m: 5512ft *refreshments, camping*). Although the village is not seen from here, this camping area is named after it, being generally known as **SOKATHUM**.

* * *

SOKATHUM - AMJILASSA

Distance:	9 kilometres (5¹/₂ miles)
Time:	4 hours
Start altitude:	1680 metres (5512ft)
High point:	Amjilassa (2590m: 8497ft)
Height gain:	910 metres (2986ft)

The lower part of the Ghunsa Khola's valley is extremely narrow and steep-walled - almost gorge-like and sliced by a turbulent river. Scant vegetation clings to the soaring walls, and waterfalls cascade in silver ribbons. The creation of a path up the north slope is a considerable achievement in itself. Not surprisingly, this first stage in the valley offers the toughest day of the trek so far, for the 910 metres of height gained between start and finish are to be achieved only by a strenuous haul up rough and sometimes greasy trails, often with quite a bit of exposure too. But there are also steep descents to surprise and disappoint, and the total amount of height-gain at the end of the day is much more than the figure above might suggest. The first time

I trekked here I reversed this route and was heartily thankful not to be going up! But in truth, once you set your mind to it and dig in, so to speak, this stage is not so bad after all. As long as you don't try to hurry, that is. But it is important to give full concentration to the trail and not allow yourself to daydream, for there are a number of exposed places where a fall could have very serious consequences - a sense of balance is essential, and no hint of vertigo.

* * *

The path to Amjilassa starts immediately from the meadowland camp and climbs quite steeply for a little over 100 metres to reach a high point of about 1795m (5889ft), where it then eases for a while, before descending a flight of stone steps. The trail then rises to a natural shelf which it follows before climbing once more.

About 55 minutes from Sokathum you cross a small landslip, shortly after which the way leads up into a vegetated cleft below a fine waterfall, continues through a belt of bamboo and a small patch of cultivation, and reaches a couple of woven bamboo houses (1hr 5mins). At the upper house the path forks (1930m: 6332ft). Take the left branch, at first up a few stone steps, then climbing in steep zigzags to the few poor houses of **GHAIYA BARI** (2125m: 6972ft

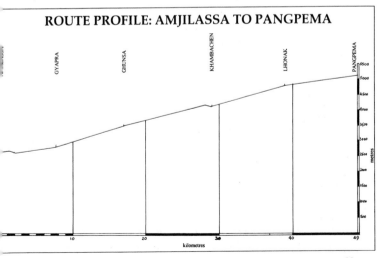

ROUTE PROFILE: AMJILASSA TO PANGPEMA

1hr 35mins).

Above Ghaiya Bari the way becomes steeper even than before, resorting to steps in places where the angle is too severe, until at about 2310m (7579ft 2 hours) a stream is crossed which, much lower down, sprays out as another of the valley's waterfalls. From this point the angle eases for a while as the trail slants across the hillside to turn a spur. Round this the way continues, gains more height, then contours to cross directly above another waterfall (2480m: 8136ft 2hrs 30mins).

Gaining more height, then rounding another spur, the path makes a steady-angled descent across the hillside before rising yet again. Another gentle descending traverse follows, then a steeper descent to a low point by a stream below yet another fine waterfall (3hrs 35mins). Now begins the rising traverse that will lead directly to Amjilassa.

Fifteen minutes after crossing the stream by the waterfall the trail takes you just below a solitary house, and 5 minutes later you arrive at the first building of **AMJILASSA**, which serves also as a teahouse and modest shop.

AMJILASSA (2590m: 8497ft 3hrs 55mins *refreshments, camping*) is a small settlement of about six houses inhabited by Bhotiya people of Tibetan origin. Camping is possible on the small terrace opposite the first house, and a little beyond this where the hillside is shallow enough to accommodate further open terraces. There are enough buildings here to house porters overnight.

* * *

AMJILASSA - GYAPRA

Distance:	8 kilometres (5 miles)
Time:	3-3½ hours
Start altitude:	2590 metres (8497ft)
High point:	Gyapra (2790m: 9154ft)
Height gain:	200 metres (656ft)

A shorter, and in many ways a less demanding, stage than yesterday's, this makes a very pleasant trek as the trail is for the most part much improved

*by comparison with the route to Amjilassa. There's also much more
vegetation, with forest sections too and a hint of bigger mountains ahead.
And more and more waterfalls in view. The way still climbs and loses
height with some frequency and with an occasional exposed section, but in
all it's a rich and varied stage to enjoy, and one which the porters will also
appreciate as it's somewhat easier than yesterday's efforts. Note that if you
are following the route on the Mandala map, that sheet gives the trail
between Amjilassa and Phere (Phole) as being on the east bank of the river.
It is not. This same map, and the Nepa sheet too, also places Kyapra
(Gyapra) on the wrong bank.*

* * *

Away from the houses of Amjilassa the path maintains a high route
well above the Ghunsa Khola by making a steady slanting ascent of
hillside, then eases round a spur. As the valley curves leftwards, so
the trail loses height and enters a belt of bamboo. This loss of height
is necessary in order to pass below a band of rocks at about 2635m
(8645ft), some 45 minutes after setting out. The way then continues
to gain and lose height in succession, and after a while passes among
a mixture of bamboo, oak and rhododendron.

Rounding the bend, the valley reveals itself as a narrow, heavily
wooded, V-shaped wedge of a gorge, with silver waterfalls slicing
through the forest on the opposite side. Again you pass beneath a
band of rocks, beyond which the valley begins to open out ahead,
still forested, but with mountains coming into view wearing snow.

Almost an hour and a half from Amjilassa, the trail crosses a
stream by way of a footbridge at the base of a superb waterfall in the
heart of the forest - the waterfall cascading in a series of steps
(2505m: 8219ft). Shortly after this the way emerges to a clearing with
two simple stone shelters butting against a rock wall just above the
river. The first of these buildings serves as a teahouse.

Once again the path rises into forest and maintains an undulating
course, crossing two or three side streams, and (2hrs 20mins) comes
to a large landslide. In 1997 this had not properly settled, and
demanded some care when making a way over it. Five minutes
beyond this another tributary is crossed below yet another fine
waterfall. More streams, more forested sections and a sharp twisting
climb up a nose of hillside brings you onto a high, open shelf near

the few houses of **GYAPRA**.

GYAPRA (2790m: 9154ft 3hrs 10mins *refreshments, camping*) -
also spelt Gyapla or Kyapra - is inhabited, as are all the villages in
this valley, by Bhotiya people. A few basic supplies and bottled
drinks are on sale, and the open pasture in front of the houses makes
an ideal campsite. From here you look north-east to a higher level
of valley, with a long ribbon of waterfall pouring from that higher
section to the lower valley. High on the opposite side blackened tree
stumps can be seen; the remains of a fire which swept across the
mountain flank several years ago. Views down-valley are quite
lovely.

* * *

GYAPRA - PHOLE - GHUNSA

Distance:	9 kilometres (5¹/₂ miles)
Time:	4 hours
Start altitude:	2790 metres (9154ft)
High point:	Ghunsa (3540m: 11,614ft)
Height gain:	750 metres (2461ft)

*The trail between Gyapra and the Tibetan refugee village of Phole is fairly
rough in places, and there is very little habitation, other than one or two
temporary teahouses set beside the path. Much of the way leads through
forest, and in the autumn season this can be very beautiful - especially when
the larches have turned to gold. The route continues beyond Phole and is
drawn to the very edge of big mountain country at last. Towering over
Ghunsa, Nango Ma has an ice-crusted ridge that signals from afar and
dominates the scene on the second half of this stage, but in the next few days
this mountain will shrink to insignificance by comparison with
Kangchenjunga's near neighbours.*

* * *

On leaving Gyapra the path soon drops to a tributary stream and
becomes a roller-coaster route once more in forest, and which, about
45 minutes from the village, brings you to river level. Here the
Ghunsa Khola thrashes its way over rocks in a state of wild fury, its

Phole, a Tibetan refugee village

constant roar being a noisy companion for a while as the trail remains close alongside it. A simple teahouse/shelter has been erected at about 2930m (9613ft). This is reached in 1hr 10mins from Gyapra.

Now the trail climbs above river level, and little over a half-hour later comes to a small stone-built teahouse (1hr 45mins). Just beyond this you cross a huge landslide, then climb steeply above the Ghunsa Khola, crossing rock slides and twisting among rhododendron, juniper and larchwoods before a short, steep climb brings you to a higher level. Another simple teahouse, this one in a flat area of larch, pine, juniper and berberis, is reached at about 3240m (10,630ft). Here the valley has opened, with broad yak pastures stretching ahead. Across these you come to **PHOLE** (3250m: 10,663ft 2hrs 45mins *refreshments, camping possible*), which some maps call Phere.

This is a long, scattered village of Tibetans who fled here in 1959 following the Chinese invasion of their country. It has strong links with Ghunsa, some of whose villagers descend to Phole for the winter. The houses are built of stone and timber, their shingled roofs

Handmade carpets and rugs are a speciality of Phole

held down with rocks. There are several teahouses, a *gompa*, mani wall and a water-driven prayer wheel at the far side of the village, which lies at the northern end of the pastures. The villagers make very fine carpets and rugs, examples of which are invariably spread out by the trail to tempt passing trekkers.

Outside Phole the valley curves north-eastward, while a tributary flows from the Nango La which is above and to the north of the village. (This pass offers a way over the mountains to the Yangma Khola, another of the valleys explored by Hooker in 1848. It was by this pass that he entered the valley of the Ghunsa Khola.) Outside Phole the trail enters an alpine region from which Nango Ma, the mountain backing Ghunsa, is seen to good effect. Half an hour after leaving the village cross the tributary stream whose wooden bridge is festooned with prayer flags. Over a rib you then enter splendid woods of larch and rhododendron, the trail contouring high above the Ghunsa Khola which is digging a trench below an impressive moraine. Gentians grow beside the path, while some of the route leading to the Sinion La can be detected on the opposite flank.

The first tentative view of Ghunsa is gained 3¹/₂ hours after leaving Gyapra. Shortly after this you pass below the abandoned village *gompa*, cross the river on a wooden cantilever bridge, and wander up a slope to enter **GHUNSA**[1] by a *chorten*.

GHUNSA (3540m: 11,614ft 3hrs 50mins *accommodation, refreshments, camping*) is the main village of the valley. Similar in style to Phole, it is quite clearly a Bhotiya settlement (the people call themselves Sherpas) built among yak pastures and potato fields outlined with drystone walls and wooden fences. Prayer flags slap from poles on practically every house; hens, chicks and yaks roam among the alleys. There are several shops, a simple lodge and a police check-post, and two or three possible campsites. It is from this village that two routes strike off across the eastern wall of mountains into the valley of the Simbua Khola, by which the south side of Kangchenjunga is reached.

Points of Interest Along the Way:

1: GHUNSA In 1962 the village was described by Jean Franco, in *At Grips with Jannu*, as being "the end of the world ... A few dozen families live there in total isolation all the year round, among their potato-fields, yaks, goats and sheep. The climate is harsh indeed and life at its most miserable." Yet when Smythe was here with Dyhrenfurth's International Expedition in 1930, his impression was more favourable, for he spoke of "a trim little place, with neatly laid-out fields." He wrote about the headman's house: "Built of sturdy timbers, with a wide-eaved roof weighted down with large stones," and of the *gompa* containing "dozens of little lockers filled with sacred books."

When I was last in Ghunsa the *gompa* was abandoned and sadly falling into a dangerous state of disrepair. But compare that with the description by the pundit, Sarat Chandra Das, who visited in 1879:

"The Tashichoding Monastery ... contains about eighty monks, besides a dozen nuns who generally reside in the village. The monastery is one of the finest and richest in Sikkim and Eastern Nepal. It contains a complete collection of the Kah-gyur (Buddhist Scriptures) and the Tan-gyur (Shastra or religious works). The Lamas wear their hair in flowing locks like lay people; they also wear long ear-rings in imitation of the early Indian Buddhists. They belong to the Nyinma-pa, or Red-Hat sect. The great Buddhist Lama (Lha-chen-chempo) who introduced Buddhism into Sikkim ... entered by this route, and established the Gyunsar Monastery."

* * *

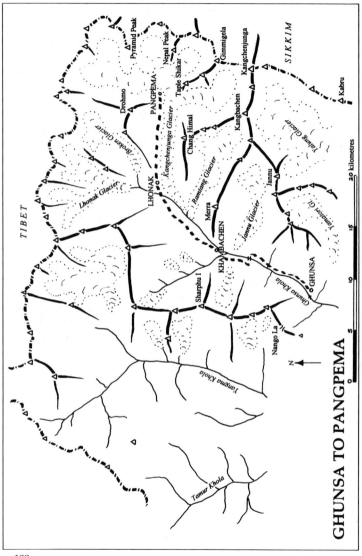

GHUNSA TO PANGPEMA

TIME SPENT IN GHUNSA

Ghunsa is high enough to be aware of the need for acclimatisation, so unless each member of the group is fit and unaffected by the altitude, it is advisable to spend two nights here before moving on. Some may welcome a rest day, doing no more than relaxing in the sunshine with a good book; others might enjoy the opportunity to explore the village and its surroundings, while perhaps the best way to acclimatise is to wander further upvalley and return to Ghunsa for the night, or follow the trail either up towards the Sinion La, or on the way to the Lapsang La.

1: Upvalley: Simply follow route descriptions for the next stage (Ghunsa-Khambachen) as far as you feel comfortable, and return by the same trail. There are teahouses beside the bridge which crosses the Ghunsa Khola, 2hrs 5mins upstream, and another 10 minutes beyond that at Rambuk Kharka on the west bank.

2: Sinion La Trail: The trail begins by the village school, which is located on the edge of an open pasture at the southern end of Ghunsa. The path rises among juniper, rhododendrons and berberis towards the mouth of a tributary glen, and in 13 minutes it forks. Continue ahead on the right branch (the left-hand trail goes to the Lapsang La) and 2 minutes later the path forks once more. Take the right-hand branch again and cross a footbridge over the Yamatari Khola into a pleasant meadow. The way continues into forest and climbs steeply to gain the crest of a ridge spur adorned with prayer flags at about 3980m (13,058ft). This is reached after about 1hr 20mins. This is a great viewpoint, for you overlook not only the lower Ghunsa Khola Valley below Phole, but also upvalley towards Khambachen.

3: Lapsang La Trail: Follow directions as given for the Sinion La Trail above, but at the first fork (13mins) bear left to climb through forest. A little over an hour from the point where you left the Sinion La trail come to a stream, which is crossed, then continue up to a yak pasture. Jannu can be seen from the top of a moraine wall banking the Yamatari Glacier at around 4000m (13,123ft).

* * *

One-time gompa *building at Ghunsa*

GHUNSA - KHAMBACHEN

Distance:	12 kilometres (7¹/₂ miles)
Time:	4 hours
Start altitude:	3540 metres (11,614ft)
High point:	4225 metres (13,862ft)
Height gain:	685 metres (2247ft)

The full dramatic grandeur of the Kangchenjunga massif becomes evident on this stage of the trek, for on the way to Khambachen an astonishing view is afforded of Jannu's tremendous north-west face soaring out of its deep glacial valley. It is without question one of the most awe-inspiring of big mountain vistas of Nepal, to stand comparison with practically anything seen in the Khumbu.

    The early part of this walk is quite gentle, but it becomes more demanding as you progress towards Khambachen, and there is one particular section which crosses a wide and unstable landslide that is both taxing and potentially dangerous. It may be advisable to have one or two people stationed at strategic points to give warning of any stonefall as you cross. It is also important to take note of any difficulties of acclimatisation suffered by group members from now on, and be prepared to act accordingly.

* * *

For the first time the route follows the east bank of the Ghunsa Khola, soon leaving the village behind. Before long a side stream is crossed on stepping stones, and caution is needed when these are glazed with ice, which is quite likely on an autumnal morning. Ahead lies an extensive area of rhododendron, juniper and larch trees, and an occasional fenced yak pasture. After 40 minutes cross a landslip and 5 minutes later descend to the sandy bed of the valley. The trail climbs out again and passes through more larchwoods and open scrub slopes.

In the spring of 1930 Frank Smythe trekked along this trail on his way to attempt Kangchenjunga with G.O. Dyhrenfurth's expedition. He was clearly enchanted by it:

"It was a delightful walk. The path lay through pine woods and glades yellow with primulas. Pine tops vignetted glimpses of cathedral-like peaks ... Alpine beauty on a loftier, nobler scale, its paths traversed only by yaks and their herds."

(F.S. Smythe: *The Kangchenjunga Adventure*)

About 1hr 25mins from Ghunsa a very fine view is gained of a rock spire upvalley, and an impressive moraine wall bulldozed by the unseen Kumbhukarna (Jannu) Glacier which appears to be almost blocking the valley with its towering cliffs of rubble. In another 5 minutes the trail cuts down to cross another landslide, descends to the valley bed again, then climbs out once more among woods of yew and rhododendron - an enchanting place. Emerging from these the trail descends yet again to the valley bed and across a wilderness of bleached stones with a bridge spanning the Ghunsa Khola seen ahead.

A teahouse stands beside the bridge (2hrs 5mins *refreshments*), but the continuing trail crosses the river and heads upstream for a further 10 minutes before reaching another teahouse at **RAMBUK KHARKA** (3900m: 12,795ft 2hrs 15mins *refreshments*). Beyond the *kharka*, or high pastureland, the path makes steady progress, gaining height towards the moraine wall seen earlier. Twenty minutes from Rambuk Kharka cross a side stream coming from a slender waterfall, then climb to another pasture. From here the way becomes steeper, rising in zigzags up a scrub-covered hillside with the moraine wall off to the right, before easing round a spur to reach a huge landslide (2hrs 50mins). This is still active, and when overnight frost has melted rocks can come bounding down with little or no warning. It is important to advance with caution. The trail makes a rising traverse that takes about 10 minutes before you reach comparative safety. Do not bunch up when crossing, but allow plenty of space between group members, and have one or two people keeping watch as you cross.

Once over the landslide danger you gain a magnificent vantage point from which to study Jannu[1] and its sharply defined glacial valley off to the right. The peak actually comes into view whilst you are crossing the landslide, but you should ignore all temptations to stop until you are on safe ground.

This is how Freshfield saw it when descending the valley during his circuit of Kangchenjunga in 1899:

"From this point the whole of Jannu was visible, in outline an enormous dome of rock, vast in bulk, symmetrical in form, and crowned by an admirably proportioned lantern. Behind it a curtain of white cliffs, closing in the head of the glacier which had formed the dyke across the lower valley, ran back towards the unseen Kangchenjunga. We looked right up the ice-stream, and down on its surface, a succession of dunes of granite débris... The view was sensational. We felt the rare rapture of the adventurer who has discovered something worth all his pains."

(D.W. Freshfield: *Round Kangchenjunga*)

The path continues to rise until, gaining a high point of about 4225m (13,862ft), still with Jannu's sheer face demanding much attention, the way contours before dropping to the lone yak herder's hut of **LAKEP** (4175m: 13,698ft'3hrs 25mins). Above this the trail crosses a spur starred with edelweiss, and slopes down to a view of **KHAMBACHEN**[2], which is reached about 15 minutes later.

KHAMBACHEN (4175m: 13,698ft 3hrs 40mins *camping*) is the summer grazing settlement of villagers from Ghunsa, located at the mouth of a tributary glen drained by the Nupchu Khola. Views to the upper face of Jannu and its icy neighbours are splendid, especially at sunset.

Points of Interest Along the Way:

1: JANNU (7710m: 25,295ft), as mentioned earlier, was first climbed by the south ridge in 1962 by a French expedition led by Lionel Terray, while the great face which is seen on the approach to Khambachen rises some 3200m (10,499ft) above its glacier. When Smythe looked at it in 1930, he considered it unclimbable. "Nothing I have seen is more hopelessly unassailable than the terrific sweep of its northern precipices," he wrote. However, the face *was* climbed in 1977 by a large expedition which managed to place four teams on the summit - a total of thirteen Japanese and three Sherpas. It has since been climbed several times, most impressively, perhaps, by Tomo Cesen in April 1989, when he made a fast solo ascent of the north face in just 23 hours.

2: KHAMBACHEN In 1879 Chandra Das visited the village, and in his *Narrative of a Journey to Tashi-lhunpo* he mentions a watermill by the stream used for milling barley that was being cultivated there. He described the houses, built of wood with gable-ends and roofed with long planks.

"No nails or ropes are used to fasten the planks to the rafters or to each other, but they are kept in their places by blocks of stone laid on them. The interior is far from uncomfortable; the windows are very small, and the houses consequently dark; but as the natives live chiefly out of doors, and always keep a fire lighted indoors, they suffer little inconvenience on this account."

The villagers were in festive mood and making a *"grand offering to the Kang-chan peak... The firing of guns, athletic feats, and exercises with the bow and arrow form the principal parts of the ceremony, which is believed to be highly acceptable to that mountain-deity."*

A few years later, in 1884, the pundit Rinsing (Rinzin Namgyal) arrived in Khambachen: *"The village at the junction of two rivers called the Thonak and the Thongchen containing pakka houses, was found empty on account of the cold season* [he arrived on 9 November], *and was surrounded by barley fields. ... There is a scarcity of firewood and grass."*

During his circumnavigation of Kangchenjunga, Freshfield came down-valley from his crossing of the Jonsang La, and also found it deserted. *"We looked down upon a village of substantial stone huts, very similar to those found in the Graian Alps. Flags and shrines lined the zigzags that led down to them. Beyond lay some level fields and meadows through which a clear and tranquil stream flowed between mossy unravaged banks. The opposite hill was clad in a grove of dwarf alders. ... But there was no sign of life, no sound audible above the murmur of the streams. The flocks had descended, the scanty crops had been reaped, and the hamlet was as desolate as an alp in winter."* Smythe was dismissive of it, writing of the "evil-smelling, refuse strewn main street of Kangbachen," and the "evils of intermarriage [which] soon manifested themselves" - describing several crétins among the inhabitants, "stunted, dwarf-like and seemingly possessed of but little intelligence."

* * *

TIME SPENT IN KHAMBACHEN

Once again it is necessary to consider the rate of acclimatisation of all members of the party. At over 4000m the altitude of Khambachen is high enough to affect some trekkers so, as at Ghunsa, it may be advisable to spend a second night here. Two acclimatisation day walks are possible.

1: Upvalley: Follow directions given for the next stage leading to Lhonak. There are several pleasant meadows along the way in which to relax with good views, but the best place to aim for is Ramtang Kharka at about 4615m (15,141ft). This gives a direct view up the Ramtang Glacier to the huge north-west face of Kangbachen (7903m: 25,928ft). Ramtang is reached about 2hrs 15mins from Khambachen village.

2: Nupchu Khola Valley: Simply wander as far into this tributary glen as you feel confident to go. Impressive views will be enjoyed there.

* * *

KHAMBACHEN - LHONAK

Distance:	10 kilometres (6 miles)
Time:	3¹/₂-4 hours
Start altitude:	4175 metres (13,698ft)
High point:	Lhonak (4815m: 15,797ft)
Height gain:	640 metres (2100ft)

Another magnificent day's trekking, this stage provides awesome views practically every step of the way as you are drawn deeper into the high Himalayan landscape. Although the trail is good for the most part, there are a few rough sections, including a boulder tip which has to be crossed, and a scree slope or two to traverse. But there are also yak pastures through which icy streams meander, and on occasion the crossing of these can be problematic. In acknowledging the amount of height to be gained by the time you reach Lhonak, a reminder is given to watch for signs of altitude (mountain) sickness - see the paragraphs relating to this under On-Trek Health in the Introduction.

* * *

Departing Khambachen the path slants up the steep wall under which most of the houses are protected; there is a *chorten* and a string of prayer flags where the trail turns the spur, and you then make a traverse of the left-hand wall of the valley with frontier peaks seen far ahead. After 45 minutes the way leads down to the valley bed where you wander ahead with a big moraine wall on the right.

In 1hr 15mins come to a scree and rock tip, after which you are faced with a section of boulder-hopping with a fine waterfall crashing down the left-hand wall just beyond. This, according to Chandra Das, is known as Khan-dum-chu, the 'fairy waterfall', whose waters are said to be sacred. The way becomes increasingly barren with more screes, rocks and small streams. Some 2hrs 15mins from Khambachen, however, you reach the broad open yak pasture of **RAMTANG KHARKA** (4615m: 15,141ft), with the Ramtang Glacier spilling out of a corrie to the right backed by the vast ice-sheathed face of Kangbachen[1].

Ahead, on the east side of the valley, an impressive rock finger projects from the lower slopes of Wedge Peak (Chang Himal). This stands almost opposite Lhonak, with the Kangchenjunga Glacier[2] flowing between. It will take about an hour and a half to reach Lhonak from Ramtang.

Crossing the near-level pasture there is a small stream to negotiate, and at the far end the way rises gently to a higher level, always keeping well to the left of the lateral moraine hiding the Kangchenjunga Glacier. The valley grows wilder as you wander through an avenue of high mountains.

After 3 hours you top a high point of moraine, from which the glacier is seen stretching far ahead to yet more outstanding mountains blocking the valley in the north-east, where they form the borders of Tibet and Sikkim. From this high point descend to cross a torrent coming from the north, then up the opposite bank where the trail winds round to an important tributary glen coming from the left. This glen is broad and flat at its entrance and is drained by a winding stream that takes the waters from three glaciers: the Lhonak, Tsisima and Broken Glacier. A short way up this glen it branches either side of Tsisima Peak (6390m: 20,965ft), and it is thought that Chandra Das crossed into Tibet by one of these branches in 1879.

The trail slopes down the moraine and brings you to three stone hutments at the yak pasture known as **LHONAK**[3] (4815m: 15,797ft 3hrs 40mins *camping*). At least one of the hutments is used as a simple lodge by porters. Mountain views are stunning in every direction.

Points of Interest Along the Way:

1: KANGBACHEN (7903m: 25,928ft), also spelt Khambachen, forms part of the lofty western ridge system of Kangchenjunga, and was for a long time considered to be that mountain's fifth summit, its north-west face looming over the Ramtang Glacier. After attempts were made by expeditions from Yugoslavia (1965) and Japan (1973), the summit was eventually gained by a Polish team via the west ridge in May 1974.

2: THE KANGCHENJUNGA GLACIER bulldozes its way down-valley to Ramtang, while moraine walls provide ample evidence of its former journey which extended to Khambachen. Unlike the majority of glaciers seen in the European Alps, the valley glaciers of the Himalaya are often so covered with debris that the uninitiated could be forgiven for believing there was no ice at all. The Kangchenjunga Glacier is a prime example of this. As Smythe commented: "This stony camouflage has ... often led travellers, and even surveyors, into the mistake of thinking that Himalayan Glaciers are much shorter than they actually are."

3: LHONAK is not only the name of the *kharka* at the confluence of the tributary glen below Tsisima Peak and the Kangchenjunga Glacier, but it also refers to a valley system in Sikkim on the north-east side of the Jonsong La - a 6145m pass at the head of the valley above Pangpema. The pundit Rinsing marked the *kharka* on his 1884 map as Lanok (his report mentioned there being a 'cattle-shed' here), but Freshfield dismissed this name as being likely to confuse, and instead called it Ramthang - the name which subsequently appeared on the map drawn by Edmund Garwood. The 1930 International Expedition to Kangchenjunga camped here and also called it Ramthang where there was a group of huts.

* * *

LHONAK - PANGPEMA

Distance:	10 kilometres (6 miles)
Time:	2¹/₂-3 hours
Start altitude:	4815 metres (15,797ft)
High point:	Pangpema (5140m: 16,864ft)
Height gain:	325 metres (1066ft)

Given sufficient time, settled weather conditions, and assuming all the party are fit and acclimatised, a camp at Pangpema can be rewarding. However, it is a very cold site and unless porters are suitably equipped to withstand the sub-zero temperatures expected overnight, a better option might be to spend a second night at Lhonak and visit Pangpema as a there-and-back day-trip. This should be perfectly feasible for a fit party - allow about 2 hours for the walk back down to Lhonak.

Scenically, this is a truly magnificent stage, with one huge mountain after another demanding attention. Throughout, the way leads alongside the Kangchenjunga Glacier, mostly in the ablation valley where Tibetan snow cocks are sometimes seen (and heard) scurrying after one another. Expect snow patches and glazed streams on the way, and in the event of mists appearing in the valley, you should stay close together, for there are a few 'featureless' sections where it would be easy to stray from the correct route. Although this final stage of the trek to the base camp area is not particularly demanding, the altitude will no doubt make itself felt.

* * *

Moving on from Lhonak the trail leads roughly eastward through a gentle area of scant grassland dotted with boulders on the north bank of the Kangchenjunga Glacier. After a while the faint trail takes you onto the moraine wall itself, from which you gaze directly onto the rubble-strewn ice that makes a moat along the base of several fine snowpeaks.

Having traced the moraine crest, the trail then rises a little to cut round a series of shallow gullies, then returns to the moraine wall. After about 1hr 10mins slope down into a trough. This is sandy at first, but as you progress through it, so it becomes increasingly rocky and barren. Boulder-hopping, you gain height with the aid of cairns to show the way, and then come onto an open flat meadow noted for a large and prominent boulder standing up at about 5025m (16,486ft 1hr 35mins). This is a glorious place with impressive mountains all around.

Beyond this meadow the way rises to cross a stone desert - again cairns guide the way. More yak pastures follow, but still no sign of Kangchenjunga which remains hidden by its neighbours. But after crossing a low grassy rib with a natural shelf below, the trail makes a traverse above this shelf and Kangchenjunga[1] slowly begins to reveal itself ahead to the right. Continuing over more grass-covered spurs, about 2¹/₂ hours from Lhonak the basin of **PANGPEMA**[2] is seen below. Five minutes later you reach the base camp site with its few low walls and a simple *chorten* - and a direct view across the glacier to the towering north-west face of the world's third highest mountain, built upon massive ice-bound terraces.

PANGPEMA (5140m: 16,864ft 2hrs 35mins *camping*) slopes down towards the Kangchenjunga Glacier, while a short distance further upvalley the Ginsang (Jonsong) Glacier[3] spills from the

Beyond Lhonak the trail to Pangpema treads moraines of the Kangchenjunga Glacier

north. Seen from here Kangchenjunga itself is framed by Gimmigela[4] (The Twins) and a spur of Chang Himal (Wedge Peak)[5], while Nepal Peak, Pyramid Peak and many others create a fabulous snow- and ice-coated backdrop upvalley. In 1899 Freshfield and his party camped just above Pangpema, "on a green shelf between the mountain and the trunk glacier, which was hemmed in on three sides by mighty snow-peaks... It is situated at a point where the glacial drainage of the greater part of the north-western face of Kangchenjunga unites with that of the chain extending to the north as far as the Jonsong Peak... It is, I fear, impossible to convey to the reader any notion of the general effect [of the landscape]," he wrote. "The individual features ... were not unfamiliar to mountaineers; the Himalayan giants are, with a difference, greater Alps; a glacier is always a glacier; but the scale was far larger and the impression left on the mind one of stupendous vastness... It is no wonder that the Nepalese yak-herds who penetrate to this spot should regard it as the special haunt of the Spirits of the Mountains, a place where 'Gods and Saints dwell in great numbers'."

Points of Interest Along the Way:

1: KANGCHENJUNGA (8586m: 28,169ft) was first climbed from the south-west (Yalung Glacier side) in 1955. Although Freshfield, studying the mountain with a seasoned mountaineer's eye, considered that the best chance of success was to be had via the North Col, all the early attempts, apart from the 1930 International Expedition led by G.O. Dyhrenfurth, were made either from the Yalung side, or via the Sikkim flank. But it was Dyhrenfurth's team which first made a serious attempt from the north-west, based at Pangpema. They were turned back when an ice avalanche killed one of their Sherpas, and no other expedition looked at this flank until Doug Scott's four-man team succeeded in 1979.

2: PANGPEMA was used as the base camp site for Dyhrenfurth's 1930 expedition, the low rock walls which stand today having been built at that time, and in 1979 Doug Scott found some old wooden tent pegs used nearly fifty years previously. It is a dramatic place with stunning views in all directions. Joe Tasker described it as "a windswept shelf of grass poised above the Kangchenjunga glacier." Scott said it was "a good place, with lots of blue sheep, birds in their winter plumage and lammergeyer higher up."

3: THE GINSANG (JONSONG) GLACIER provides the key to the Jonsong La, the 6145m (20,161ft) pass leading into Sikkim crossed in the reverse direction by Freshfield in 1899, and from south to north by Dyhrenfurth's expedition in 1930. Smythe suggested that once you turn the corner at Pangpema you enter a "different country and a different climate ... the strong, dry winds of Thibet protect the Jonsong Glacier to a large extent from many of the snowstorms that attack Kangchenjunga."

4: GIMMIGELA (7350m: 24,114ft), dubbed 'The Twins' by Freshfield, is a double peak (the east summit is 7004m: 22,979ft) situated on the Nepal/Sikkim border just to the north of Kangchenjunga's North Col. It was only made available to mountaineers by the Nepalese government in 1994 and was climbed for the first time by a Japanese expedition in October of that year, the ascent being made from the Sikkim side via the east ridge. The second ascent of Gimmigela was achieved in October 1995, this time from the Nepalese side by way of the south-west ridge by a large team of eleven Japanese and five members of the Nepalese Police Force, together with twelve climbing Sherpas. Out of this large climbing force, the summit was gained by seven Japanese and ten Nepali climbers. A British Services expedition made the third ascent in May 1997, also via the south-west ridge.

Freshfield was the first mountaineer to describe Gimmigela from Pangpema. This is what he wrote: "Though separated from Kangchenjunga by a broad snowy saddle [the North Col], it may be considered a buttress of the greater mountain... From its summit a long spur projected towards us, crowned by several snowy domes or half domes. It ended in a curiously jagged, low rock-ridge that from some points of view serves as it were for a footstool to the great white throne above." (*Round Kangchenjunga*)

5: WEDGE PEAK (6750m: 22,146ft), named Chang Himal by the Nepalese, is the beautiful ice-fluted peak whose extending spur forms the western gatepost to Kangchenjunga's north-facing corrie. "Other mountains may be termed fanged, or sugar-loafed," wrote Smythe, "but the Wedge Peak seen from the north is nothing more or less than a gigantic elemental wedge. It is a brutal mountain ... its very aggressiveness challenges the mountaineer to pit himself against it, yet what mountaineer would accept the challenge? ... Turn to the skyline. There ice, not ordinary ice, sharp-edged and unbroken, but ice hacked and tortured by the winds, clings to the ridges; thin flakes of ice through which the sun gleams with a cold fire; pinnacles of fairy-like delicacy, elegant busts, daring minarets, extravagant mushrooms, a strange goblinesque procession, drunken and tottering, frozen in a downward march." (*The Kangchenjunga Adventure*)

* * *

TIME SPENT AT PANGPEMA

Unless you plan to return the same day to Lhonak, the hillside north of Pangpema will reward with even more spectacular views than may be had from the base camp area. About 220m (722ft) above Pangpema, and reached by way of the crest that edges the Ginsang Glacier, there is a natural shelf that acts as a grandstand from which to view Kangchenjunga's vast face.

You could push further upstream along the Ginsang Glacier's moraine bank to gaze on other peaks too. But there are several opportunities to fill a few hours of scenic rambling from Pangpema. Just be aware that often cold winds sweep upvalley, bringing low clouds and poor visibility during the afternoon.

* * *

PANGPEMA TO GHUNSA

Having been as far as trekkers are allowed to go on the north-west side of Kangchenjunga, it will be necessary now to return down-valley. Assuming the plan is to cross the dividing ridge into the valley of the Simbua Khola, and from there visit the south-west (Yalung Glacier) side of Kangchenjunga, Ghunsa will be your destination. From a camp at Pangpema you should allow two days for this: the first as far as Khambachen, the second to Ghunsa itself. Neither stage will be too demanding. However, if you visited Pangpema on a day-trip from Lhonak, one day should suffice to return to Ghunsa from that camp.

In the event of bad weather preventing a crossing of the ridge, allow about seven days to return to Dobhan from Lhonak, plus another day from there to Suketar if you plan to fly out from Taplejung.

If, however, your plan is to return to Basantpur or Tumlingtar, allow ten or eleven days for the trek from Lhonak.

* * *

TREK 2:
GHUNSA TO THE VALLEY OF
THE SIMBUA KHOLA

"The path up the ascent was blocked with snow-beds, and for several miles we alternately scrambled among rocks and over slippery slopes, to the top of a ridge of rocks running east and west from a superb sweep of snowy mountains to the north-west, which presented a chaotic scene of blue glacial ice and white snow, through which splintered rocks and beetling crags thrust their black heads."

(Joseph Dalton Hooker: *Himalayan Journals*)

The ridge that divides the valleys of the Ghunsa Khola and Simbua Khola consists of an impressive spur of mountains some 40 kilometres (25 miles) long, running south-west from Kangbachen and Jannu, narrowing as it does until it plunges to the Tamur between Hellok and Sokathum. From Kangbachen to the Yamatari Glacier this ridge is impassable to trekkers, but there are two routes, traditionally used by local yak herds and traders, that exist just to the south of this glacier. These cross the Lapsang La (5258m: 17,251ft) - a difficult route often obscured by deep snow - and a lower series of passes, the Sinion La (4660m: 15,289ft), Mirgin La (4675m: 15,338ft) and an unnamed pass at about 4720m (15,486ft).

Neither of these routes should be taken lightly. Both enter remote country from which escape could be difficult or dangerous in the event of bad weather, and although the Sinion La-Mirgin La route has a visible trail in good conditions, there are sections that could be very confusing in mist and / or snow. In places the Lapsang La route has no trail at all, and a knowledgeable guide is essential in finding the way as it crosses yak pastures and tackles steep moraines, a glacier and boulder slopes in the shadow of Jannu and Boktoh.

The lower route only will be described. For this crossing two days should suffice. It starts in Ghunsa and ends at the yak *kharka* of Tseram, and adds a certain *frisson* to the trek. This is the route used by Hooker in 1848. He called it the Choonjerma Pass, as did the pundit Chandra Das when he crossed in the opposite direction in June 1879.

* * *

GHUNSA - MANI BHUK

Distance: 5 kilometres (3 miles)
Time: 3 hours
Start altitude: 3540 metres (11,614ft)
High point: Mani Bhuk (4290m: 14,075ft)
Height gain: 750 metres (2461ft)

It may be feasible for fit and strong trekkers to complete the crossing to Tseram in one long (very long) day. But it would be impossible for laden porters. It is of course far more enjoyable to take two days. The route is an attractive one, albeit steep and demanding in places, but being acclimatised after spending a few days above 4500 metres, all the effort required should be quite acceptable.

* * *

The crossing begins by the village school at the southern end of Ghunsa's open pastureland, where a clear trail climbs a slope among juniper, rhododendron and berberis, heading towards the mouth of a tributary glen - that of the Yamatari Khola. In 7 minutes cross a minor

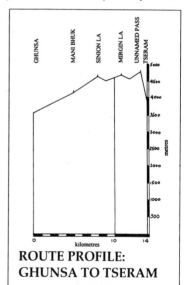

ROUTE PROFILE: GHUNSA TO TSERAM

116

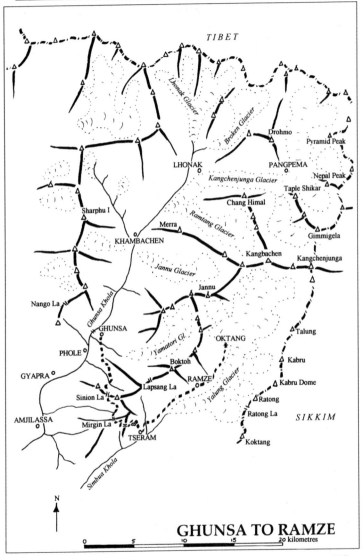

GHUNSA TO RAMZE

stream, and when the path forks 6 minutes later, take the right-hand option. (The alternative is the start of the Lapsang La trail.) At the next trail junction (15mins from the start) continue ahead and cross the Yamatari Khola by footbridge to enter a lovely meadow. Over this the way goes into a forest of tall juniper and rhododendron trees.

This is an enchanting forest, the mature trees wrapped in thick coatings of moss, and with tatters of lime-green lichen dangling from the branches. On coming to an open patch a fine view is afforded along Ghunsa's valley towards Khambachen. The way climbs steeply on, and eventually emerges from the trees to a brief crest adorned with prayer flags at 3980m (13,058ft 1hr 20mins). Although it is not a true pass, it is known locally as the **TAMA LA**. From this idyllic spot one can gaze not only down the length of the valley of the Ghunsa Khola, and up it, but also across to the Nango La and the mountains which divide Ghunsa's valley from that of Yangma.

"At last we gained a bare brow, a rib of rock and turf, forming the angle of the mountain between the Yamatari glen and the valley of Kangchen. Prayer-flags marked this as a 'La'. This term is applied not only to a pass but to any distinct stage in the day's journey, any place inviting burdened men to repose and meditation. The top of any steep slope may therefore be called a La. The coolies were not remiss in seizing the occasion."

(D.W. Freshfield: *Round Kangchenjunga*)

The path does not cross this rib, but climbs up it, soon providing a bird's-eye view down to the toy-like houses of Phole, before contouring across the right-hand slope of the ridge which effectively separates the Yamatari glen from the Ghunsa Valley. The contour becomes a rising traverse, climbing here, descending a little there, but generally gaining height across the mountainside with consistently fine views down the southern end of Ghunsa's valley to a blue wash of distant foothills.

Then the trail cuts into a scoop where the ridge curves in a steep little corrie-like indent, topped by an obvious saddle. Just below the saddle there is a good water supply (2hrs 15mins) - the first since the Yamatari Khola, 2 hours before. Trekking groups often stop here for lunch.

Climb in steep zigzags to gain the saddle (4210m: 13,812ft 2hrs 25mins), beyond which the trail continues to rise to mount a ridge projection 60 metres higher. This provides access to a large corrie that plunges into a narrow glen far below. The path, which is a good one now, crosses the head of this corrie on a long undulating traverse, mostly on grass slopes. But after crossing a large clutter of rocks you come to the lovely grass basin of **MANI BHUK**[1] (4290m: 14,075ft 3 hours *camping*).

Points of Interest Along the Way:

1: MANI BHUK is a charming little meadow fringed with rocks and boulders. A clear stream idles through before chuntering beneath the boulders and disappearing down-valley. When I first came here it was a pristine area. Now it boasts a couple of rough, temporary shelters used as teahouses run by Tibetans. It makes an ideal campsite. Freshfield noted signs of it having been used as a camping ground in 1899, and in 1848 Hooker came upon a family of Tibetan shepherds here:

"Further on we reached an open grassy valley, and overtook the Tibetans, who had halted here to feed their sheep. A good-looking girl came to ask me for medicine for her husband's eyes, which had suffered from snow-blindness: she brought me a present of snuff, and carried a little child, stark naked, at nearly 14,000 feet elevation, in December! I prescribed for the man, and gave the mother a bright farthing to hang round the child's neck, which delighted the party. My watch was only wondered at; but a little spring measuring-tape that rolled itself up, struck them dumb, and when I threw it on the ground with the tape out, the mother shrieked and ran away, while the little savage howled after her."

(Joseph Dalton Hooker: *Himalayan Journals*)

As a postscript to Hooker's story, Chandra Das's account of his journey to Lhasa in 1881 mentions that one of his guides, by the name Phurchung, happened to be the 'little savage' given the coin by Hooker. Phurchung remarked to Chandra Das that he considered himself especially fortunate, for although other mothers and children begged Hooker for similar gifts, the great man gave them nothing.

* * *

MANI BHUK - TSERAM

Distance:	9 kilometres (5¹/₂ miles)
Time:	4-4¹/₂ hours
Start altitude:	4290 metres (14,075ft)
High point:	Unnamed pass (4720m: 15,486ft)
Height gain:	430 metres (1411ft)
Height loss:	850 metres (2789ft)

Of the three passes crossed on this stage of the trek, confusion reigns as to which La is which. Some authorities claim that the first is the Mirgin La, the second being the Sinion La. Others argue that the Sinion La is the first to be crossed, while Bezruchka also names this Menda Puja. The Ghunsa man who accompanied my last crossing called the first La, the Sinion La, the second the Mirgin La and said that the third, unnamed, pass was called the Deorali Danda - but this is a common Nepali name which merely indicates the ridge-top of a hill. (In 1881 Chandra Das called it the Nango Lap-tse.) As if this were not enough, Hooker referred to the Mirgin La as the Choonjerma Pass - but, according to Chandra Das, Choonjerma (meaning 'collection of cascades') is the rocky terrace between the Mirgin La and the unnamed pass. Chandra Das also refers to yet another pass between the 'Seenon-La and Mirkan-La' as the Pangbo La. All very confusing!

It's quite a tough stage, which ends with a very steep descent to the Yalung (Simbua Khola) Valley. Given good visibility there are long views to Jannu, Makalu and the Khumbu peaks, and from the final pass a tremendous introductory view of Kabru, Ratong and the Yalung Glacier.

* * *

Across the stream at Mani Bhuk the trail to the Sinion La climbs into an upper corrie ringed by minor peaklets to cross a rock-cluttered landscape, through which a stream drains mostly beneath the rocks. About 25 minutes from Mani Bhuk the path follows the course of this stream uphill for a while, making towards an obvious saddle above and to the right. As you gain height, look behind you to catch sight of Jannu appearing over an intervening ridge.

The Sinion La (4660m: 15,289ft)

"Looking north, the conical head of Junnoo was just scattering the mists from its snowy shoulders, and standing forth to view, the most magnificent spectacle I ever beheld. It was quite close to me, and is much the steepest of all the peaks of these regions."

(Joseph Dalton Hooker: *Himalayan Journals*)

"The crests of Jannu and its two attendant peaks, just visible over the dark ridge in the foreground, gave a splendid promise and foretaste of the view that awaited us. At every upward step they rose more boldly and defiantly above the intervening crags."

(D.W. Freshfield: *Round Kangchenjunga*)

The trail takes you over two or three false cols before slanting up to the prayer-flag festooned **SINION LA**[1] (4660m: 15,289ft 1hr 20mins), a ridge projection adorned with cairns, from whose highest part (to the right of the actual pass) you may be able to recognise Makalu, Lhotse Shar, Mount Everest, Chamlang etc. in a long line of snowpeaks to the north-west, while a last view of Jannu is granted to the north-east.

Leaving the pass the trail veers left below the ridge, and descends a little to a fork, reached in about 7 minutes from the Sinion La. Take the left-hand path which makes a gentle descending traverse before rising again, just as gently, on a very stony route that eventually leads to another ridge spur (1hr 50mins), from which you see round the head of a corrie to the Mirgin La. On the approach to this pass, note a prominent Sphinx-like rock standing proud above you. This was commented on by Hooker (*"a curious isolated pillar"*), Chandra Das (*"the rock resembled the head of a horse looking towards the Kang-chan"*), and by Freshfield (*"a strange obelisk"*).

The **MIRGIN LA**[2] (4675m: 15,338ft 2hrs 20mins) is a saddle marked with cairns and a pile of rocks sprouting prayer flags. From it the route descends a short distance, then veers left to pass beneath a large overhanging rockface. (Just before this is reached an alternative trail descends to a pair of small lakes, and from there continues down to the lower valley of the Simbua Khola, which it reaches about 3 hours downstream of Tseram.)

Passing below the overhanging rocks the main route follows a long traverse on a rocky terrace cutting across a steep slope. The traverse rises in order to gain, then cross, the final (highest) pass of the route, the **UNNAMED PASS**[3] (4720m: 15,486ft 3 hours). This too is marked with prayer flags, and from it a stunning panorama encompasses much of the upper Yalung Valley - the Yalung Glacier, Ratong, Kabru and the huge snowbound crest leading to Kangchenjunga. Kangchenjunga is not seen from this point, however, apart from a brief hint. Across the deep valley to the south-east runs the Singalila Ridge, marking the border with Sikkim.

Briefly traverse left, then descend to another ridge spur with cairns and prayer flags, and from there continue over a clutter of rocks on the descent to the Yalung (Simbua Khola) Valley. On coming to a viewpoint overlooking a small tarn, the descent begins in earnest and is very steep. Caution is required, especially when the trail is glazed with snow or ice, in which case porters may need assistance. The first of two tarns is reached 20 minutes or so after crossing the final pass. According to Chandra Das these tarns are called **TSHO CHHUNG DONKA**, and are said to be presided over by two mountain deities.

Pass round the left-hand shore of the first to reach the second, smaller, tarn. Round the right-hand end of this the descent resumes.

The unnamed pass provides a grandstand view of Talung,
Kabru and Ratong

It's a steeply plunging trail, with the Tseram meadows in sight for much of the way. Towards the foot of the slope wind through cypress woods and come to the yak pasture of **TSERAM** (3870m: 12,697ft 4hrs 15mins *camping*), set above the north bank of the Simbua Khola.

TSERAM has become an important camping area on this south side of Kangchenjunga. Between my first two visits a lot of scrub had been cleared away to enlarge the campsite, and now there are two buildings, one of which acts as a very basic lodge with a few items of food and drink for sale. Across the valley to the south-east is a glen which is topped by the glacier pass of the Kang La (5054m: 16,581ft), by which traders, and some early mountaineering expeditions, entered Nepal from Sikkim. "From a scenic standpoint the Kang La is not an attractive pass," according to Smythe, who crossed it in 1930 with the International Expedition to Kangchenjunga. The pass is not seen from Tseram, however.

Points of Interest Along the Way:

1: THE SINION LA was praised for its views by both Hooker and Freshfield. The latter spoke of the "loose stone-men and the waving prayer-flags that crowned the ridge."

"The outlook from my 'coign of vantage' was prodigious both in extent and splendour and in the marvellous variety of light and of shadow, of atmosphere and of colour. ... I was perched at an altitude of 15,300 feet, on one of the south-western spurs of the Kangchenjunga Group, the snows of which I, as it were, touched. On one side rose its majestic walls and towers of rock and ice; on the other I overlooked all Eastern Nepal, the valleys of the Tambur and Arun and their tributaries, and the southern borderland of Tibet."

(D.W. Freshfield: *Round Kangchenjunga*)

2: THE MIRGIN LA was reached by Hooker as the sun was going down (he had begun his crossing that morning) and he was guided for much of the subsequent descent by the moon. But in describing the view from this pass, the great botanist was inspired to wax lyrical:

"As the sun declined, the snow at our feet reflected the most delicate peach-bloom hue; and looking west from the top of the pass, the scenery was gorgeous beyond description, for the sun was just plunging into a sea of mist, in a blaze of the ruddiest coppery hue. As it sank, the Nepal peaks to the right assumed more definite, darker, and gigantic forms, and floods of light shot across the misty ocean, bathing the landscape in the most wonderful and indescribable changing tints. While the luminary was vanishing, the whole horizon glowed like copper from a smelting furnace, and when it had disappeared, the little inequalities of the ragged edges of the mist were lighted up and shone like a row of volcanoes in the distance. I have never before or since seen anything which for sublimity, beauty, and marvellous effects, could compare with what I gazed on that evening from Choonjerma pass."

(Joseph Dalton Hooker: *Himalayan Journals*)

In 1930, Frank Smythe was less fortunate:

"We reached the Mirgin La ... under a greying sky. Hailstones were falling, and from the east came an occasional thunder growl. Below, the snow slopes fell away into a desolate valley, ribbed with ancient moraines, like the

embankments of a railroad fallen into disrepair. A few tattered prayer flags fluttered on the summit of the pass. Viewed thus under a leaden sky, with light and shadow merged into one universal monotone, black-jawed crags jutting from livid featureless snow slopes, and a chill wind sighing through the gap, it was a depressing scene."

(F.S. Smythe: *The Kangchenjunga Adventure*)

3: THE UNNAMED PASS, as mentioned above, was called the Nango Lap-tse by Chandra Das in the narrative of his 1881 journey to Lhasa. In a passing reference to its crossing he mentions making "the usual votive offering of a few scraps of rags inscribed with the *mantras Lha sol-lo, Lha kyal-lo* ('God be praised, God be praised')".

* * *

Fit and well-acclimatised trekkers could make a there-and-back day's journey from Tseram to the viewpoint of Oktang, from which the south-west face of Kangchenjunga is seen to such impressive effect. But for preference, and assuming time is not pressing, a better plan would be to trek next day to the yak pasture of Ramze ($2^1/_2$ hours) at 4615m (15,141ft), make a camp there, and spend the next day leisurely exploring the way to Oktang along the big moraine wall of the Yalung Glacier.

These routes will be described in detail below, under Trek 3: Kangchenjunga South. (Please turn to page 143.)

* * *

TREK 3:
KANGCHENJUNGA SOUTH

"We travelled ... through an immense variety of country and people, flora and fauna: terraced hillsides, friendly Hindu, Buddhist and Tibetan villages, dense and unspoilt forests of bamboo, rhododendron and ancient pine, and steep gorges cut by powerful mountain torrents. Then, above the treeline, there were yak pastures, desolate moraine-covered glaciers and, on the hillsides, occasional herds of wild blue sheep, the whole dominated by some of the most spectacular mountain vistas in the world."

(George Band: *Alpine Journal 1996*)

Accompanied by Joe Brown, George Band made the first ascent of Kangchenjunga in 1955 via the Yalung Glacier. Forty years later he took part in a nostalgic return to the mountain, and the above quotation is taken from his account of that trek, in an article entitled *Kangchenjunga Revisited 1955-1995*. As Band enumerated, such are the pleasures in store for trekkers tackling this route.

Options available for the trek to the south side of Kangchenjunga are several and varied:

✗ 1:   From Basantpur to Dobhan (already described under Trek 1: Kangchenjunga North Base Camp), and from there to Suketar, the STOL airstrip for Taplejung, to join the main route listed under option 3 below.

✗ 2:   From Tumlingtar to Dobhan (also described under Trek 1: Kangchenjunga North Base Camp), and from Dobhan in a steep one-day climb to Suketar to join the main route.

✓ 3:   Flight to Taplejung (Suketar) followed by six or seven days of tough cross-country trekking to reach Tseram in the valley of the Simbua Khola below the Yalung Glacier. And from there head upvalley to Oktang in full view of Kangchenjunga's huge south-west face.

4: By road to Ilam and on to Gopetar, where a trail heads north into the valley of the Kabeli Khola and joins the main trek at Yamphudin.

The trek from Taplejung (Suketar airstrip) will be described. This offers the shortest route, and is one that is adopted by many groups. The flight comes from Biratnagar, and is invariably made during the morning before afternoon winds or cloud build-up make landing at Suketar's short meadowland strip too hazardous. It's an exhilarating flight which leaves Biratnagar at an altitude of only 72 metres (235ft), and lands at Suketar's 2400 metres (7874ft). Eventually Taplejung will be served by road, and flights may then be in less demand than they are today.

From the airstrip the trek heads roughly north-east, crosses the forested Surkhe Danda and descends through terraced fields to the deep valley of the Phawa Khola. Here a suspension bridge leads to a steep climb through Kunjari to gain another *danda* with views towards Kangchenjunga. Now the route passes many small villages scattered amongst cultivated terraces that seem to step every hillside. Rice, millet, small fields of wheat or sweetcorn, bananas and oranges, all help create rich patterns and textures, while knuckle indents are tree-clad, their sides running with small waterfalls and streams. Crossing ridge spurs with much height gain and loss every day, the trek comes to the valley of the Kabeli Khola and remains high above the river on the west flank, following a magical belvedere with hinted snowpeaks ahead.

Just before reaching Mamankhe a long suspension bridge takes the trail over a gorge-like tributary, and from Mamankhe to Yamphudin it's very much a roller-coaster route, still above the Kabeli Khola. Yamphudin itself is approached through cardamom plantations at river level, but thereafter the vegetation changes. There are no more villages, as such, and the landscape takes on a wilder appearance as the trek leaves the Kabeli Khola, crosses a heavily wooded ridge and descends to the Omje Khola. Then begins a long, and at times, a steep climb through rhododendron forest to another ridge crossing at Lamite Bhanjyang. Huge landslides have rearranged the northern side of the pass, but once across these the way plunges down to the Simbua Khola - the river valley which drains the Kangchenjunga massif.

A day's walk upstream leads to Tseram and the first near-views of the Himalayan giants. Then on to small glacial lakes and yak pastures, huge moraine walls and the 'spectacular mountain vistas' referred to by George Band, a crescendo of ice-plastered faces and lofty ridges creamed with billowing cornice. Ramze is usually the highest camp, at about 4615m (15,141ft). This yak pasture is located in a broad ablation valley at the point where the Yalung Glacier makes a sharp elbow curve between shapely Ratong and Boktoh, and from it a morning's walk leads to a *chorten* built upon the moraine wall from which Kangchenjunga's imposing face makes a stunning backdrop.

* * *

As with the trek to the north-west side of the mountain, it is essential that porters and all crew members are properly clothed and equipped to combat the sub-zero temperatures that must be expected at the highest camps. Ramze is well above the timberline, and all cooking must be done on kerosene stoves - that includes food for porters too. In regard to food, groups must be self-sufficient throughout the trek, for villagers along the route produce no more than their own basic needs.

* * *

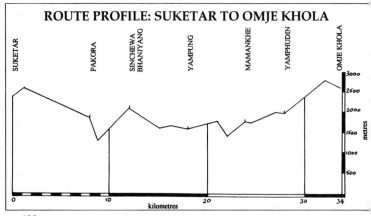

ROUTE PROFILE: SUKETAR TO OMJE KHOLA

Mani Bhuk, en route to the Sinion La (Trek 2)
Jannu, as seen from the Sinion La (Trek 2)

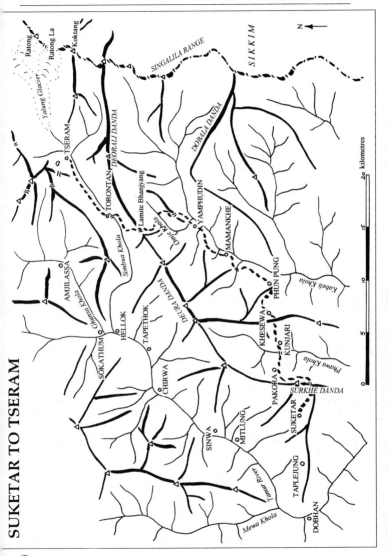

SUKETAR TO TSERAM

Ratong
Ratong La
Koktang
Yalung Glacier
TSERAM
SINGALILA RANGE
SIKKIM
DEORALI DANDA
TORONTAN
Simbua Khola
Lamite Bhanjyang
Omje Khola
DOBALA DANDA
YAMPHUDIN
AMJILASSA
Ghunsa Khola
HELLOK
TAPETHOK
SOKATHUM
DEURA DANDA
MAMANKHE
PHUN PUNG
Kabeli Khola
CHIRWA
KHESEWA
KUNJARI
Phawa Khola
SINWA
MITLUNG
PAKORA
SUKETAR
SURKHE DANDA
Tamur River
TAPLEJUNG
Mewa Khola
DOBHAN

20 kilometres

N

Tseram

129

SUKETAR TO RAMZE AND OKTANG

The flight to Taplejung (Suketar) takes half an hour from Biratnagar in the eastern Terai - a brief but exciting journey which leads from one world to another. Biratnagar itself is reached by air from Kathmandu (daily flights take one hour), or by a long day's drive by bus - the airport is 4 kilometres north of the town. In theory it should be possible to leave Kathmandu on an early morning scheduled flight, and make a connection for the Biratnagar-Taplejung link in order to begin trekking from Suketar the same day. Such is the theory. Just bear in mind that planes only fly to Taplejung in the morning, so it's quite likely that a delayed take-off from Kathmandu could mean a missed connection in Biratnagar, resulting in a day's wait in that hot and bustling town.

Taplejung airstrip is located high above the township after which it is named, beside the Tibetan village of Suketar. This village has developed into something of a shanty, with poor lodges and a collection of shops selling bottled drinks. Camping is possible on a patch of land next to the gompa, with tremendous introductory views of the distant Kangchenjunga range.

* * *

SUKETAR - PAKORA

Distance:	8 kilometres (5 miles)
Time:	3-3½ hours
Start altitude:	2400 metres (7874ft)
High point:	Surkhe Danda (c.2655m: 8711ft)
Height gain:	255 metres (837ft)
Height loss:	715 metres (2346ft)

For a first day's trek this makes a good introduction to the area, for there is a variety of scenes to enjoy, and a good trail to follow. There are forested sections, open meadows, terraced hillsides and neat houses dotted across the landscape. A strong party starting early could continue beyond Pakora - maybe even going as far as Kunjari on the eastern side of the Phawa Khola - but it's better to ease gently into this trek for there will be some tough days ahead.

* * *

Brush-maker on the Surkhe Danda above Suketar

Above Suketar a broad track/dirt road cuts across the hillside towards a long rhododendron-covered ridge. This track should be followed as far as a left-hand bend where a minor path breaks away directly ahead. Rising among trees and shrubs, the path brings you onto the actual crest of the **SURKHE DANDA**, then you wander along the crest, sometimes among rhododendrons, sometimes across open grassland, before descending a flight of stone steps to a saddle and a five-way junction of paths marked by a small Hindu shrine. There are two buildings here, one of which is a teahouse.

Bear right on a trail which contours, then descends through forest, crossing several streams along the way. A gentle uphill rise, still in forest, brings you to a ridge spur, and over this you descend again out of the trees and soon come to a lone house and a storage barn at **LAL KHARKA** (c.2300m: 7546ft 2hrs 15mins). A short distance below this a rough terrace on the right of the trail suggests a possible campsite.

The path returns to woodland, descending still, then along an easy contour among bushes and trees, crossing more streams until turning a spur by a *chautaara* at about 2190m (7185ft). Round this spur the path continues to lose height, sometimes quite steeply, then less so with terraces curving round the hills and the shadowed valley of the Phawa Khola seen far below.

The trail is obvious, and it brings you to the scattered village of **PAKORA** (1940m: 6365ft) which boasts a school. Camping is possible here.

* * *

PAKORA - YAMPUNG

Distance:	10 kilometres (6 miles)
Time:	4¹/₂-5 hours
Start altitude:	1940 metres (6365ft)
Low point:	Phawa Khola (1430m: 4692ft)
High point:	Sinchewa Bhanjyang (2135m: 7005ft)
Height gain:	705 metres (2313ft)
Height loss:	c.900 metres (2953ft)

After an early descent to the Phawa Khola, a long climb leads through the Limbu village of Kunjari to a saddle on a ridge, followed by a contour round to a second saddle in which the houses of Sinchewa Bhanjyang enjoy long views to Kangchenjunga and Jannu. There are other ridge spurs to cross as the trek continues its undulating course over this high foothill country, more forested sections too, through which a succession of lovely waterfalls cascade. It's a land of lush cultivation and strung-out villages providing the human dimension, and although it makes quite a tough stage, it is without doubt a rich and rewarding one.

* * *

Descending below Pakora you soon pass through terraced fields to **SIMBU**, which has a shop beside the trail, and then down to the Phawa Khola where, about half an hour from the start, a suspension bridge at 1430m (4692ft) takes you across to the east bank. Now begins the steep climb to **KUNJARI** (c.1800m: 5906ft), a village set among terraces covering a difference in altitude of nearly 200 metres. There are shops, and a school which draws children from a very wide area, and the village holds a monthly market. Sometimes groups camp in the school yard. Flanking the village masses of terraced fields, and groves of banana and bamboo, provide colour and interest.

Above Kunjari a variety of trails gradually converge as one on the final ascent to a ridge spur on which a *chautaara* has been set on the very summit. Now bear left on a slightly descending trail which soon contours to a second spur with another *chautaara*. This is at about 2080m (6824ft), and the group of houses on the Sinchewa Bhanjyang can be seen ahead. The continuing trail slopes down to a waterfall in a wooded gully, then rises to **SINCHEWA BHANJYANG** (2135m: 7005ft *refreshments, camping possible*), a rather scruffy Gurung village nestling in a saddle from which lovely views show the Kangchenjunga massif in the distance. At a junction of tracks near a collection of shops and teahouses, bear left. Crossing the saddle the path rises a little among trees and shrubs, then slopes down to **KHESEWA** (1955m: 6414ft), reached about 25 minutes from the *bhanjyang*. Like Kunjari, Khesewa is also built on various levels amidst terraces of rice and millet in a large amphitheatre of hills.

From here the way maintains a steady slanting descent, enters woodland and crosses a stream (the Nangden Khola) on a log bridge - some care may be needed on this. The hillside is heavily forested, and the trail loses, then gains a little height, passes below an open slab streaked with cascades, closely followed by a beautiful slender waterfall coming down a deep green groove with a shallow pool at the bottom. Immediately after this the path climbs to yet another *chautaara* and resumes its undulations.

There are more waterfalls, streams, and a few houses, as the trail makes its way round to a ridge spur which contains the northern side of the amphitheatre. Gathered on, or just below, this spur nestle the few houses of **PHUN PUNG** (1845m: 6053ft) - shown as Fun Fun on some maps. On gaining this point you enter the major valley of the Kabeli Khola.

Once again the landscape ahead and below displays an amazing array of terraces, and the trail cuts alongside many of these, then slants down across the hillside towards another village, bigger yet more scattered than Phun Pung and with a series of small waterfalls

The trek to Kangchenjunga passes many memorial stones like this one.
Often these are built into chautaaras

tipping down the hillside above it. This is **YAMPUNG** (1720m: 5643ft), which is also known as Anpan, Anpang or Yangpang. Camping is possible here on terraces near one of the waterfalls.

* * *

YAMPUNG - MAMANKHE - YAMPHUDIN

Distance:	10 kilometres (6 miles)
Time:	4-4¹/₂ hours
Start altitude:	1720 metres (5643ft)
High point:	Pumpe (1875m: 6151ft)
Height gain:	c.455 metres (1493ft)

Traversing high above the Kabeli Khola, this stage makes a superb trek, full of visual stimulation and cultural interest. But it's not all easy walking, for the hillside is broken by a few tributary streams, one of which breaks out of a glen and the path descends steeply to cross on a suspension bridge - then, of course, it's necessary to regain much of the lost height. Later there are deep indentations that require more height loss and gain, so the roller-coaster nature of the trek is maintained. Of the villages visited on this stage, Mamankhe is the best, with a number of charming thatched houses, some with carved wooden balconies hung with flowers that would not seem out of place in Switzerland. At the end of the day Yamphudin sits at a confluence of valleys, and permits will need to be checked at the police post.

* * *

The day begins with a rising traverse that takes you above the last houses of Yampung, and rounding a spur with a *chautaara*, you are treated to a view of Jannu peering above a distant ridge. The valley of the Kabeli Khola stretches ahead as a deep cleft filled with morning shadow. Now the path makes a comfortable belvedere, at the end of which another *chautaara* marks the start of the descent into the mouth of the Takshewa Khola tributary glen. At the head of this tributary rises Megnug (3903m: 12,805ft), the high point of the Deura Danda.

Before the descent into the glen steepens, you come to a huddle of houses and shops. This is the settlement known as **PUMPE** (1875m: 6152ft *refreshments*) - or Phonpe. Passing through, the trail comes to a fork where you bear right and descend steeply among shrubs and trees, then below a few terraced fields and houses, before coming to the long suspension bridge spanning the Takshewa Khola. Beside the bridge a cascade pours from the vegetated slopes

Suspension bridge between Pumpe and Mamankhe

into the river below. The bridge is about 300 metres below Pumpe, and once across it the path twists up, soon reaching more terraces and a few houses. Poinsettias hang above the trail.

The way continues among fertile terraces and arrives at the prosperous Limbu village of **MAMANKHE** (1840m: 6037ft 2hrs 15mins) near the school. It will take a good half-hour to walk through this village. On the way you'll pass one or two teahouses and simple shops, and as you leave the last houses of Mamankhe the trail goes through a small meadow which makes a fine campsite with a water supply just below.

Once again the trail slopes into an indent with a stream flowing through. Stepping stones offer a way across when the stream is low, otherwise a suspension bridge of questionable safety suggests an alternative method. The path then angles up the hillside and turns a spur at about the same height as Mamankhe. The spur is marked by a *chautaara*, a *chorten* and prayer flags, and from it lovely views back show Mamankhe settled among its fertile terraces.

For the next hour and a half or so, the trek continues its undulating course high above the Kabeli Khola. The trail is mostly good, and the only real alternative to beware of is when a secondary trail breaks off to descend to a suspension bridge seen straddling the Kabeli Khola itself. Although there are possibilities for camping on the east bank of the river just short of Yamphudin (another bridge at the far end of the village enables you to return to the west bank), it is better to remain on the left-hand side of the river.

Not long after you have passed above the suspension bridge, the main trail descends among trees, winds through a lush growth of cardamom and soon after comes to the edge of **YAMPHUDIN** (2000m: 6562ft *refreshments, camping*). Immediately before reaching the village a trim meadow fringed with trees suggests a good campsite between a side-stream and the Kabeli Khola.

YAMPHUDIN is the last village on this trek to the south side of Kangchenjunga. Settled by a mixture of Limbu, Rai and Bhotiya people, it stands at the confluence of the Kabeli Khola and Omje Khola. On my first visit the recent monsoon had wreaked havoc when the Omje Khola burst its banks and washed away several houses and fields. Huge boulders and landslides of mud destroyed sections of the village, uprooting trees and burying crops.

Yamphudin today has a large school, a few simple shops and a police post. In addition to rice, millet and corn, crops of cardamom are grown here, while just outside the village, on the north side of the Kabeli Khola, you may see so-called rice-paper being made, the sheets spread out in the sunshine to dry on wooden frames.

* * *

YAMPHUDIN - OMJE KHOLA

Distance:	6 kilometres (3 miles)
Time:	3 hours
Start altitude:	2000 metres (6562ft)
High point:	Dhupi Bhanjyang (2780m: 9121ft)
Height gain:	780 metres (2559ft)
Height loss:	c.280 metres (919ft)

Between Yamphudin and the valley of the Simbua Khola there are two ridges to cross. The first rises north of the village and effectively divides the headwaters of the Omje Khola from the upper Kabeli Khola. The second is the long Deorali Danda which lower down becomes known as the Deura Danda. The crossing of these ridges breaks this part of the journey into two stages, and although the first is short, it's energetic enough - especially in full sunshine. To reach the Dhupi Bhanjyang a long zigzag trail rises up the south-facing hillside largely without shade, and is then followed by a steep and rough descent through dense forest to the banks of the Omje Khola - the river that enters the Kabeli Khola a short distance from Yamphudin campsite. In the autumn of 1997 a new path had been made most of the way to the pass, but the northern side was narrow and rough as it twisted beneath snagging branches of trees, creating difficulties for laden porters. But it is quite possible that by the time this guide is published, an improved trail will have been made for this descent.

* * *

Towards the northern end of Yamphudin cross the Omje Khola on a bridge made of bamboo poles, pass one or two more houses and curve left, ignoring a suspension bridge over the Kabeli Khola. A few minutes later cross another tributary, beyond which the path begins to rise up the hillside. It's a clear and obvious route, passing a few houses then twisting, sometimes steeply, sometimes on wood-braced steps, up the vegetated hillside in full sunshine. This can be a very hot and tiring ascent, and is best tackled in the cool of morning.

The crest of the *danda* is reached at a saddle known as **DHUPI BHANJYANG** (2780m: 9121ft), and almost immediately you enter jungle-like forest which clothes the northern slopes. Hopefully the path will have been improved by the time this guide is in use, otherwise the descent will be steep and greasy, and bullied by trees.

The path brings you down to the south (true right) bank of the Omje Khola, at about 2500 metres (8202ft), then you scramble along the bank heading upstream for a while. On my last trek along here, fallen tree-trunks had to be climbed over, others ducked beneath (no fun for porters carrying *dokos*), and muddy banks slithered on. On coming to a wooden bridge, cross to the north bank and climb up to a levelled camping area on a shelf above the river. Named after the river this is known as **OMJE KHOLA** (2610m: 8563ft). The site is a good one, and with some shelter provided for porters. The campsite also has a teahouse/shop, but the owner doesn't bother to keep it stocked, so on no account rely upon buying anything here.

* * *

OMJE KHOLA - LAMITE BHANJYANG - TORONTAN

Distance:	9 kilometres (5¹/₂ miles)
Time:	4-4¹/₂ hours
Start altitude:	2610 metres (8563ft)
High point:	Lamite Bhanjyang (3520m: 11,549ft)
Height gain:	910 metres (2986ft)
Height loss:	470 metres (1542ft)

This is the toughest stage so far, with a long, steep climb to the Lamite Bhanjyang on the crest of the notoriously damp and misty Deorali Danda, followed by another steep descent to the Simbua Khola valley. The ridge is heavily clothed in rhododendron forest, and in the early summer it must be magnificent. From a point on the ridge above the pass a view can be obtained on the proverbial clear day of Jannu, Kangchenjunga and Kabru. On the northern side of the ridge two huge landslide scars prove a daunting prospect, especially as the descent path crosses both, although it is said there is an alternative way down which avoids this potential danger. Once down from the ridge you at last enter the valley which will lead all the way to Kangchenjunga, and make a camp in a poor clearing above the river.

* * *

Immediately on leaving the terraced Omje Khola campsite the trail climbs steeply up the hillside, passes to the right of a simple farm shelter and enters bamboo thickets and woodland with a few open glades. Having gained about 500 metres (1640ft) of height the trail crosses an open *kharka* (grazing area) with a small shelter off to the right of the path. This is known as **CHITRE** (1hr 15mins) and it

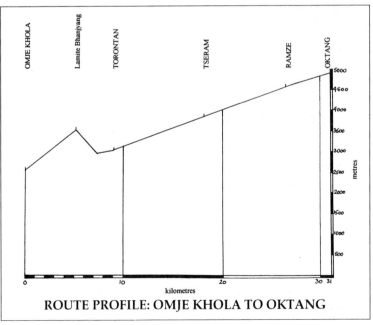

ROUTE PROFILE: OMJE KHOLA TO OKTANG

offers the only opportunity for camping between the river and Lassi Than just below the ridge crest. There is only room for a few small tents, and water is a long way off, yet it is sometimes used by trekking parties.

The continuing ascent resumes among trees, twisting steeply and with only brief snatches of views out towards Yamphudin and the valley of the Kabeli Khola. There is little respite, but the rhododendrons and pines which crowd the trail give the route a hauntingly attractive air. Long ribbons of lichen and dense carpets of moss indicate plenty of moisture, and damp mists often hang for days at a time among the trees.

Just below the crest of the Deorali Danda you emerge from forest to a rough pasture in which you will find a simple stone-built shelter. This is **LASSI THAN**. There is plenty of room here in which to camp, but again the nearest water is located about 20 minutes below to the south-east. The saddle of Lamite Bhanjyang is a couple of minutes ahead. From it Jannu is seen rising above intervening ridges, but if you have energy to spare and conditions are right, it might be worth bearing left up the ridge for a half-hour or so to gain a viewpoint in a clearing from which Kangchenjunga is also on show.

On gaining the saddle of **LAMITE BHANJYANG** (3520m: 11,549ft 2hrs 15mins) bear right and go up the ridge a short distance to a point at which the trail crosses to the north side and overlooks the first of two huge landslides. At present the trail makes a traverse of both these landslides, but they appear so unsettled that it's quite possible that with another monsoon or two, the route might well become impassable here. But I am reliably informed that a safer alternative exists. Instead of crossing the ridge by the landslide continue heading east along the crest until a zigzag descent takes you down the left-hand slope and eventually links with the main route. The gradient eases, the trail becomes wider but is likely to be greasy after rain or heavy mist, and it winds among more forests, these now of fir and bamboo, down towards the valley of the Simbua Khola.

About 300 metres below the Lamite Bhanjyang wander through a clearing with a simple house set beside the trail. The descent continues, sometimes steeply, but more often at a steady angle, crosses a stream and eventually comes to the left bank of the Simbua Khola. The way now heads upstream for a while among bamboo and wild raspberries until reaching a wooden bridge spanning the river at a point where it narrows between huge smooth boulders (3050m: 10,007ft). Cross here, and go up the slope to a rough area used by groups as a campsite a few metres above the river.

This is **TORONTAN** (3060m: 10,039ft). There are no buildings, but there is a large overhanging boulder just to the right of the trail, and tents can be fitted in a somewhat ad hoc manner among the trees.

* * *

TORONTAN - TSERAM

Distance:	9 kilometres (5½ miles)
Time:	3½-4 hours
Start altitude:	3060 metres (10,039ft)
High point:	Tseram (3870m: 12,697ft)
Height gain:	810 metres (2657ft)

The Simbua Khola drains the Yalung Glacier which flows from Kangchenjunga, and the route upvalley will lead in a couple of days into the very heart of the massif. On this initial stage a first near view will be enjoyed of Kangchenjunga's neighbours, though not of the big mountain itself. That will only be seen once the yak pasture of Ramze has been passed. From the valley's heavily-wooded gorge-like narrows at Torontan, the trail keeps to the north bank all the way, much of it leading through continuing forest, but with alpine-like sections in which the head of the valley is revealed. Although there are only a few steep ascents, it's a reasonably tough, if short, stage, and some trekkers might begin to feel the effects of altitude.

* * *

For a while the trek goes through almost primeval forest; dead trees lie where they have fallen, rocks and boulders are camouflaged by thick mossy coats, and numerous streams cascade among the trees. The trail fights a way through this wilderness, then makes a steep

141

ascent, part of which is in the open for a change, before resuming in forest once more.

As the way progresses there will be a few minor landslides to negotiate, streams to cross on stepping stones or log bridges, and more lichen-hung trees to dodge round. Eventually come to a clearing with a solitary herder's hut at about 3590 metres (11,778ft). This is referred to as **WHATA** and some groups choose to camp here. Continuing upvalley you come to another stream crossing and a junction of trails. That which bears left climbs to the Mirgin La, one in a series of passes leading across the mountains to Ghunsa. Maintain direction with yet more forest and open glades, and a little under an hour from Whata note a small Buddhist shrine to the left of the trail. The shrine is set against a large boulder. Prayer flags and a number of cairns complete the picture, but if you study the boulder closely you may detect a couple of dark streaks that are assumed to bear the image of a snake. Beyond this point the valley is considered sacred.

For some time the trail dodges from forest to river bed and back to forest again. On those sections where you nudge alongside the forest and gaze upstream along the river bed, a distant wall of snowpeaks begins to reveal itself. Then you leave the trees and pick a way among the bleached rocks of the valley bed, before climbing up the bank to emerge at the yak pasture of **TSERAM**[1] (3870m: 12,697ft *camping*).

Points of Interest Along the Way:

1: TSERAM is the first of a series of yak pastures in the Yalung Valley used by villagers from Ghunsa. It consists of two open terraces which make idyllic campsites. There are two stone hutments, one of which presents itself as a 'hotel' - a very basic lodge with a few food items for sale. When Dyhrenfurth's International Expedition to Kangchenjunga arrived in Tseram in 1930, having crossed the Kang La from Sikkim, they found "a rude hut, long and wide-eaved, with the boards of its roof weighted down with stones." In his account of the expedition, Frank Smythe tells how he spent an evening in the hut:

"One end of it was reserved for yaks, the other end for the yakherd and his family. A mass of dirty straw, alive with fleas, was the family couch. At one

corner were piled some sacks of grain, rough cooking utensils, and wooden drinking cups. The rough and uneven floor was paved with stones and dried mud. A fire of rhododendron wood was burning on a primitive stone hearth, but as there was no chimney the smoke had to find its way out through chinks in the roof, a process more efficient in theory than in practice."

(F.S. Smythe: *The Kangchenjunga Adventure*)

In 1955 Tseram was chosen as their Acclimatisation Camp by the British expedition that went on to make the first ascent of Kangchenjunga.

* * *

TSERAM - RAMZE

Distance:	8 kilometres (5 miles)
Time:	2¹/₂ hours
Start altitude:	3870 metres (12,697ft)
High point:	Ramze (4615m: 15,141ft)
Height gain:	745 metres (2444ft)

Scenic grandeur on this stage is of the highest degree, with soaring ice-caked mountains forming a horseshoe around the valley. Still Kangchenjunga remains hidden, but Kabru, Ratong, Koktang etc. are no second best, and when seen reflected in the semi-frozen waters of a small glacial lake, they create a truly memorable landscape. Trekkers are reminded that at these altitudes it is necessary to drink plenty of liquids, and to watch for signs of mountain sickness.

Note: it should be possible for fit and well-acclimatised trekkers to achieve a there-and-back day-trip from the Tseram campsite to the viewpoint of Oktang, from which Kangchenjunga will be seen in all its splendour. But unless time is short, it is much better to take an easy day to Ramze, spend at least one night there, and visit Oktang the next day.

* * *

From Tseram the trail winds up through woodland, and coming to the edge of a deep and eroded ravine, meets an alternative path cutting off left. This offers a way up to a pair of tarns and a continuing trail leading over the ridge to gain the Ghunsa Valley. The main trail, however, eases down to cross by log bridge the stream which runs through the ravine. Climbing out on the far side, the way resumes among trees and shrubs, and about half an hour from Tseram comes to a *chorten* by a large boulder with a *mani* chipped in it. Views ahead show Kabru and Ratong.

Five minutes from the mani boulder pass a stone-walled enclosure and a pair of houses. The path then works a way along the ablation valley below the Yalung Glacier's lateral moraine, and in a little under an hour and a half you reach the lovely **YALUNG** pasture at about 4290 metres (14,075ft). This is a flat area with a sparkling stream meandering through. As you continue ahead in the ablation valley the trail makes few demands, while gaining height in short steps and with Ratong and its neighbours gaining in stature as you progress towards them.

Rising from one yak pasture to another, come to the first glacial lake at **LAPSANG** (4460m: 14,633ft 1hr 50mins). This is a magnificent site, dominated by graceful Ratong[1] (6678m: 21,909ft), which plunges to the deep cut of the Ratong La[2], then rises again onto Koktang, a 6147 metre (20,167ft) mountain noted for its beautiful ice-fluted ridge.

The way to the Lapsang La - the higher and more difficult route to Ghunsa - heads off to the left of the lake into a hinted glen where, it is believed, there formerly stood the Decherol Monastery[3]. The trail to Ramze, however, cuts along the left-hand shoreline, crosses more yak pastures and reaches a second tarn, smaller than the first, but also providing splendid views. About 20 minutes later you come to the two stone huts of **RAMZE** (4615m: 15,141ft 2hrs 30mins *camping*) - also spelt Ramche, or Ramser.

RAMZE is the uppermost yak grazing pasture in the Yalung's ablation valley, bounded by a high curving moraine wall to east and south, and overlooked from the north-west by Boktoh. As Moraine Camp for the successful 1955 expedition, 300 porters deposited six tons of food and equipment here to be ferried up the glacier to the Base Camp site near Pache's Grave at the foot of the Lower Icefall.

Suketar, with Kangchenjunga on the horizon (Trek 3)
On the trail from Tseram to Ramze (Trek 3)

Ratong (left) and Koktang - one of the great views of Nepal (Trek 3)
The vast Southwest Face of Kangchenjunga, from Oktang (Trek 3)

Ramze, in the ablation valley beside the Yalung Glacier

Despite the absence of any Kangchenjunga views, Ramze is an extremely scenic site for a camp, and it is worth spending at least two nights here, if the programme allows.

Points of Interest Along the Way:

1: RATONG towers over the Yalung Glacier at the point where the valley makes a sharp curve to the south. Shown as Little Kabru on E.J. Garwood's map in Freshfield's book, Harold Raeburn, during his visit here in 1920, suggested a better name was Rathong Peak after the pass (or La) that lies immediately below it.

2: RATONG LA is the deep saddle between Ratong and Koktang that was crossed in October 1920 by Harold Raeburn and C.G. Crawford, who discovered that the glacier flowing from it to join the Yalung was "provided with a most even and convenient high central moraine" which gave easy access to the col. The Nepal-Sikkim border is reached at the pass, and from it "the E. side opened on the enormous glacier cirque embraced by the two southerly ridges of Kabru." Raeburn wrote that it is an easy pass, by alpine

145

standards, and speculated that it had been crossed long ago by Tibetans migrating into Sikkim.

3: DECHEROL MONASTERY is referred to as Dechenrol (Raeburn) and Dechhen Rolpa (by Chandra Das). When the pundit passed through the Yalung Valley in 1881 he wrote of this monastery as being located "in the woody solitudes...on the waist of this romantic snowy mountain [Jannu]." He said there were six monks at the monastery, the head Lama being Jingma-Gya-mtsho. But when Smythe came to Tseram in 1930 and made enquiries about Decherol, he was told that it had been a ruin for thirty years or more. (Raeburn reckoned it had been ruined and deserted for about forty years, but that would contradict Chandra Das's statement.)

* * *

RAMZE - OKTANG

Distance:	5 kilometres (3 miles)
Time:	1¹⁄₂-2 hours
Start altitude:	4615 metres (15,141ft)
High point:	Oktang (4780m: 15,682ft)
Height gain:	165 metres (541ft)

When planning this short stage remember to allow plenty of time to return to Ramze (45mins) or Tseram (2¹⁄₂ hours). Although it is a short stage, and without too much height gain, the altitude will no doubt make it seem more demanding than either time or distance would suggest. But what a walk it will be! Remaining down in the ablation valley, the route soon heads north towards the upper reaches of the Yalung Glacier through an immense trough walled by towering mountains. Keep alert for sightings of a herd of bharal (blue sheep) that graze nearby on the flanks of the big snow peaks - the pad marks of the elusive snow leopard have also been reported here. As Kangchenjunga at last comes into view, the way climbs onto the moraine crest and continues ahead as one massive mountain after another reveals itself. On this, the highest stage of the trek to the south side of Kangchenjunga, you will need plenty of film for your camera.

* * *

Ramze, highest camp on the south side of Kangchenjunga

Crossing the Ramze pastures the trail soon curves leftward into the final mountain sanctuary blocked by Kangchenjunga. Yet still the mountain is hidden from view as the way rises in modest steps through the boulder-pocked ablation valley. This narrows and the trail becomes a little rough in places, the lateral moraine rising darkly to the right. Then at long last the head of the valley becomes visible, and there is Kangchenjunga, its monstrous south-west face spread right across one's line of vision, while across the Yalung Glacier to the right hanging glaciers form a long veneer of ice under the lofty summit ridge connecting Kabru[1] and Talung[2]. To the left crags, broken mountain slopes and snowfields foreshorten all views. In the autumn trekking season there is little avalanche activity to worry anyone wandering to Oktang, but during the Kangchenjunga Reconnaissance of 1954, John Kempe found that in the middle of May an avalanche fell into the valley almost every ten minutes. (Doug Scott once claimed that in his experience Kangchenjunga is the most active Himalayan mountain in regard to avalanches.)

On reaching a large, prominent boulder in the midst of the ablation valley, head up the moraine wall to its crest. Once there you can look directly down onto the rubble-littered glacier, but do not be tempted too near the edge for in places the moraine crumbles. On the crest a narrow path projects towards Kangchenjunga which is now growing in stature.

Eventually this path brings you to a *chorten* topped with prayer flags. This is **OKTANG** (4780m: 15,682ft), and it makes a splendid viewpoint from which to study a great collection of high mountains: Kangchenjunga[3], of course, with the Upper Icefall, the Great Shelf, Gangway and Sickle being visible features made famous by the early expeditions. Then there is Yalung Kang[4] at the left-hand end of the blocking ridge, the tip of Jannu[5] high above and also to the left, while one peak after another tops the lofty wall to the right.

It is possible to continue further along the moraine wall, where Jannu becomes more evident (it looks very different from here; the familiar armchair shape, so easily recognisable from the foothills, is confused), but Base Camp itself is too far away and necessitates crossing the glacier to reach it.

Return to camp by the same route.

Points of Interest Along the Way:

1: KABRU is really a massif with several summits and/or subsidiary peaks over 7300 metres (23,950ft) stretching south along the Nepal-Sikkim border ridge between Talung and Ratong. Naming from the north, these are Kabru IV, Kabru III, Kabru North, Kabru South (or Kabru I) and Kabru Dome. In 1883 W.W. Graham claimed to have made the first ascent with the Swiss guides Ulrich Kaufmann and Emile Boss, but his account was short on detail and several leading members of the Alpine Club at the time disputed the claim. Others supported him (including Freshfield and Garwood) and the controversy built a head of steam with accusations that Graham and his party were on the wrong mountain altogether. One respected mountaineer with Himalayan experience who stood by Graham was Tom Longstaff, who provided a measured defence in the *Alpine Journal* with the words: "Now, for anyone who is a mountaineer, and has seen Kabru, it is impossible to believe that Graham, Emil Boss, and Kaufmann could make any mistake as to what peak they were on. They may have been impostors, but they could not have been mistaken; my point is that we have no tittle of evidence to show that they were either." (T.G. Longstaff: Six Months' Wandering in the Himalaya *AJ* vol. 31) If Graham did climb Kabru, then this was the highest summit reached for many years.

2: TALUNG (7349m: 24,111ft) was attempted from the Yalung Glacier in 1954 by John Kempe, John Tucker and Gilmour Lewis following their Kangchenjunga Reconnaissance. Reaching a high point of about 7160 metres they were forced to retreat, but ten years later an international team made a successful ascent when Franz Lindner and Tenzing Nindra reached the summit via the south-west flank.

3: KANGCHENJUNGA was first tackled from the Yalung Glacier in 1905 by an expedition organised by the Swiss, Dr Jacot-Guillarmod, which included the notorious Aleister Crowley (the so-called Great Beast 666) who had been to K2 with him three years previously. At the end of August the team was camped at about 6200 metres (20,341ft), and late on the afternoon of September 1st three of the party, with three porters, set out to descend to a lower camp, after being warned by Crowley that it was dangerous to do so. Two of the porters fell, triggering an avalanche which buried four of the party under three metres of snow. Despite hearing cries of help from the survivors, Crowley remained in his tent drinking tea. "Not that I was over anxious in the circumstances to render help. A mountain 'accident' of this sort," he wrote, "is one of the things for which I have no sympathy whatever."

The south-west side of the mountain was next visited in 1920 by Harold Raeburn, who explored the head of the Yalung Glacier, visited the site of the 1905 Base Camp and examined the route to the Talung Saddle. He did no serious climbing, however, and it was 1929 before the Yalung face received another attempt. This time it was by an inexperienced American, E.F. Farmer, who had a misdirected ambition to make a solo ascent of Kangchenjunga. He was last seen on May 27th climbing towards the Talung Saddle.

Following reconnaissance expeditions in 1953-54, a British expedition under the leadership of Charles Evans made a successful ascent from the Yalung Glacier in May 1955 when two teams reached a point just below the actual summit, having given an undertaking to the Maharajah of Sikkim not to stand on the very top - George Band and Joe Brown were first on the 25th, followed by Norman Hardie and Tony Streather the next day.

4: YALUNG KANG (8433m: 27,667ft) is Kangchenjunga's west summit. A Japanese expedition made the first ascent in 1973 via the south-west ridge, and at the same time revised various heights of the massif, giving Yalung Kang as 8505m. This reading appears today on some maps, while 8433m is quoted elsewhere.

5: JANNU is one of the most distinctive and easily recognisable of all mountains in the Himalaya of Nepal. In the autumn of 1957, Guido Magnone and two companions studied the mountain from the Yalung Glacier, and discovered ice-plastered ridges and ice avalanches thundering down at a frightening rate. Due to this, they turned their attention to the Yamatari Glacier region, from where the peak seemed almost as formidable. It was climbed via the south ridge in 1962 by a French expedition led by Lionel Terray and Jean Franco.

* * *

RAMZE TO SUKETAR

In order to return to the airstrip at Suketar, two routes are suggested. These are briefly outlined below. The first simply retraces the outward trek and could be achieved in five hard days - or six more-relaxing stages from Ramze, as follows:

1: Ramze - Tseram - Torontan
An easy route, downhill virtually throughout, and in forest for much of the way below Tseram.

2: Torontan - Lamite Bhanjyang - Omje Khola
This is a tough day with plenty of height gain and loss. It effectively reverses a stage of the outward route. The descent from Lamite Bhanjyang can prove to be tiring for the knees.

3: Omje Khola - Yamphudin - Mamankhe
A splendid day's trekking in a warm climate and with a welcome return to cultivated hillsides. Mamankhe has a fine campsite, though limited in size, at its entrance.

4: Mamankhe - Yampung - Sinchewa Bhanjyang
Strenuous, but scenically varied, the route is a true roller-coaster. Plenty of terraced countryside, plus woodland and waterfalls. The camp ground at Sinchewa Bhanjyang can be somewhat dusty.

5: Sinchewa Bhanjyang - Kunjari - Lal Kharka
A long descent to the Phawa Khola leads to an even longer climb to camp at Lal Kharka. A shorter option would be to camp at Pakora, thus making a more strenuous final day.

6: Lal Kharka - Surkhe Danda - Suketar
A final, short stage takes the trek over the rhododendron-clad ridge of the Surkhe Danda and down to Suketar for a relaxing wait for the next morning's flight out.

* * *

The second option is for a longer and more varied trek by way of the valley of the Ghunsa Khola - the valley which leads to the north-west side of Kangchenjunga described under Trek 1. Without side-tracking from Ghunsa to Pangpema, this will require about seven or eight days: two days from Ramze to Ghunsa via the Unnamed Pass, Mirgin La and Sinion La, plus five or six days from Ghunsa to Suketar.

1: Ramze - Tscho Chhung Donka Tarns

From the Ramze campsite return down-valley, but immediately after crossing the eroded ravine shortly before reaching Tseram, take the alternative path which climbs the hillside and leads directly to the two small tarns named, according to Chandra Das in the 19th century, Tscho Chhung Donka. (I have not found any mention of this name elsewhere, nor any alternative name for the lakes.) There is room for tents on the grass slope above the second of these tarns.

2: Tscho Chhung Donka - Unnamed Pass - Mirgin La - Sinion La - Ghunsa

This is quite a demanding stage, but it can be a magnificent one given good conditions, with long views and plenty of variety.

3: Ghunsa - Phole - Gyapra

After yesterday's tough crossing, this mostly gentle downhill stage comes as a pleasant surprise. Fine woodland, interesting villages and a very pleasant campsite at the end of the day set on a shelf high above the river.

4: Gyapra - Amjilassa - Sokathum

With more than 1100 metres (3600ft) of altitude to lose - and a lot of it on steep and sometimes difficult trails - this can prove to be quite a tough day's trekking. The valley of the Ghunsa Khola shows itself as a steeply-walled, wooded gorge, and in places below Amjilassa, the route is rather exposed.

5: Sokathum - Hellok - Chirwa

The valley of the Tamur River will seem blissfully warm after days spent at altitude, and on this stage terraced fields and banana trees will be seen once more. Several suspension bridges are crossed, and the trail follows an undulating course from one small village to the next.

6-7: Chirwa - Suketar

A short distance beyond Chirwa the trail forks. The lower, main path, continues along the river valley and in $1\frac{1}{2}$-2 days comes to Dobhan, from which Suketar may be reached in a further day via Taplejung. The left branch, however, slopes up the hillside and in two days leads to Suketar. Not having used that approach myself, I have no details to offer, but am assured it is a good route.

* * *

DOBHAN TO BASANTPUR

Groups who plan to trek out to the roadhead at Basantpur, rather than fly from Suketar, will arrive in Dobhan at the junction of the Maiwa Khola and Tamur River, after a week's walking from Ramze via Yamphudin and Suketar as outlined in the first option above, or in 4½-5 days from Ghunsa via Sokathum and Chirwa. From Dobhan the standard route to Basantpur reverses the trek described under Trek 1: Kangchenjunga North Base Camp - Basantpur to Dobhan. This is achieved in three or four delightful days, as briefly set out below:

1: Dobhan - Gurja
This can be a tiring stage, for it's uphill practically all the way, and in both spring and autumn seasons the temperature may be warmer than you'd like for such exertions. However, the countryside is magnificent, with cultivated terraces everywhere, and views behind you to the Kangchenjunga massif. Camp at Gurja and enjoy sunset and sunrise views over the Himalaya.

2: Gurja - Gupha Pokhari
From Gurja the trail climbs to rhododendron forest, and on to the ridge crossing at Buje Deorali. Thereafter more forest sections and another ridge or two will be tackled before dropping to Gupha Pokhari, which again enjoys distant views of the Himalaya.

3: Gupha Pokhari - Chauki
A short and easy stage, this could be achieved in a morning. It would be possible to continue to Basantpur, to make a fairly long day, but unless you are pushed for time it would be worth delaying arrival at the roadhead in order to spend a last night enjoying the alpenglow on Makalu, Chamlang and the Khumbu peaks. In any case, Chauki is much more pleasant than Basantpur.

4: Chauki - Basantpur
By delaying arrival at Basantpur until this short morning stage, it will be possible to begin the road journey to Kathmandu the same day. If the plan is to fly out from Biratnagar, that town should be reached during the evening after leaving Chauki, with a flight the following morning.

* * *

DOBHAN TO TUMLINGTAR

Another option for leaving the mountains is to trek to Tumlingtar and fly direct from there to Kathmandu. This is a splendid alternative to the well-used Suketar and Basantpur routes, with a tremendous range of cultivated land on both sides of the Milke Danda ridge between Dobhan and Tumlingtar. Allow five days from Mitlung or Dobhan.

1: Dobhan - Dhungesanghu

It will only take about 2 hours to reach camp at Dhungesanghu from Dobhan, but assuming you approach from the Tamur Valley, it is likely that you'll have spent the previous night at Mitlung. In which case the climb to Dhungesanghu will have been tacked on to a morning's walk along the lower valley. (Mitlung-Dobhan-Dhungesanghu)

2: Dhungesanghu - Milke Danda

With about 1100 metres (3600ft) of height to gain, this stage will be demanding enough. It leads at first among terraces, and later enters hillside forests before coming to a clearing below, and on the eastern side of, the Milke Danda.

3: Milke Danda - Chitlang

Crossing the wooded ridge of the Milke Danda, a long, 1700 metre (5500ft) descent takes the trek down to Nundhaki and the Piluwa Khola, where camping is possible on a riverside terrace. Yet again views of the big mountains are tremendous, even though they are now shrinking to a distant horizon. From the Milke Danda, Gupha Pokhari may be seen too, before the trail plunges downhill towards the deep river valley.

4: Chitlang - Chainpur

It may be possible to walk as far as Tumlingtar on this stage, but Chainpur is a fascinating township and it would be worth spending a few hours there. From the Piluwa Khola the way climbs at an easy angle among terraces (as ever) to gain a ridge at Tanglewa, then makes a traverse to Pokhari, and along a broad ridge-top path to Chainpur. There is a good campsite with fine distant views to enjoy.

5: Chainpur - Tumlingtar

An easy morning stroll, downhill practically all the way, leads to the Hinwan Khola where you cross either by ferry, or by wading. Tumlingtar airstrip is located on the opposite bank, set in a raised meadow on a plateau between two rivers.

* * *

KANGCHENJUNGA FROM SIKKIM

"The romantic beauty of the landscape was almost beyond belief. Looking out of the windows...on the snows of Kangchenjunga, I felt a worn-out mountaineer might be well content to spend the end of his days at Gangtok."

(D.W. Freshfield: *Round Kangchenjunga*)

The Kangchenjunga massif straddles the borders of Nepal and Sikkim, with the long Singalila Ridge stretching to the south marking the frontier between the two kingdoms. Trails along this ridge provide some of the most spectacular views to be found in any foothill country, and although Sikkim was only reopened to trekkers in 1985, this particular region has since become justly noted for its scenic and trekking qualities.

Sikkim is wedged between Nepal and Bhutan, while its northern border overlooks Tibet. Formerly an independent Buddhist kingdom, it was drawn by treaty under the protection of the British Empire in the first half of the nineteenth century, became an Indian protectorate in 1949, and was annexed as the 22nd state of India in 1975.

Bhotiyas from Tibet, Nepalese emigrants, Lepchas and Indians make up a diverse population and contribute to the region's cultural riches. Covering an area of just 7300 square kilometres (2819 sq. miles) it is India's smallest state, both in terms of physical size and population. Composed of the luxuriant Rangit and Teesta river basins, it is largely contained within a lofty system of ridges, along which the best of its treks are found. Monsoon rains fall heavier here than almost anywhere else in the Himalaya. As a result vegetation is both lush and varied, the state boasting more than 4000 flowering plants and shrubs, including bougainvillaea, magnolia, poinsettia, some 40 species of rhododendron, and 600 orchids - all of which have gained Sikkim a reputation as the 'Garden Kingdom of the Himalaya'. Animal and bird life is also abundant. As well as the red panda, barking deer, musk deer and Himalayan bear, more than 500 species of birds and 600 of butterflies have been recorded.

Designated as a restricted area, application to trek in Sikkim needs to be set in motion some time before arrival. Both an Indian visa and a special permit will be required. Adventure travel companies arranging treks will provide advice on how to obtain these, as well as vaccination requirements, and will no doubt take care of the bureaucracy involved. Independent travellers should allow at least four months in order to process the necessary applications - apply for a restricted area permit at your nearest Indian embassy or consulate, and state your wish to visit Sikkim. A trekking permit must also be obtained before entering Sikkim - unlike the Nepalese system where permits can only be arranged after arrival in Kathmandu.

Travel to the country will usually focus on Darjeeling. From the UK this will normally be by air to Delhi, an onward flight to Bagdogra (Siliguri), followed by a 3-hour drive by private vehicle (4 hours or so by public bus), through the tea plantations for which the area is noted. Travellers coming by road from Nepal should make for the border crossing at Kakarbitta, and the first Indian village of Raniganj from where you can get a bus or jeep to Siliguri (New Jalpaiguri), for the onward journey by bus or train to Darjeeling. The famed narrow-gauge steam railway is scenic but slow - the 122 kilometre (76 mile) journey taking between 8 and 12 hours. Once in Darjeeling the final spectacular stage to Sikkim can be made by bus, taxi or jeep.

Darjeeling was adopted by the British as a hill station (or sanatorium) in the 1830s, and grew rapidly with houses, barracks, a bazaar and later, hotels. "A few official residents, civil and military, formed the nucleus of a community, which was increased by retired officers and their families, and by temporary visitors in search of health, or the luxury of a cool climate and active exercise," wrote Hooker after his visit in 1848.

Kangchenjunga dominates the view from Darjeeling. "The view ... is quite unparalleled for the scenery it embraces, commanding confessedly the grandest known landscape of snowy mountains in the Himalaya, and hence in the world. Kinchinjunga (forty-five miles distant) is the prominent object, rising 21,000 feet above the level of the observer out of a sea of intervening wooded hills."

* * *

SIKKIM TREKS

Two short treks (with variations), which make the most of those views, have grown popular in recent years. The first, an easy but delightful trek, heads along the Singalila Ridge north of Darjeeling, while the second starts at Yuksom, reached via Gangtok - the capital of Sikkim - and makes for the 4940 metre (16,207ft) Goecha La. The first offers broad panoramas that include Everest, Lhotse and Makalu as well as Kangchenjunga, while the second spends much time in a deeply wooded valley before emerging to the splendours of Ratong, Koktang, Kabru Dome and a near view of (again) Kangchenjunga. This latter route is more challenging than the first, and time should be allowed in which to acclimatise properly before climbing to the Goecha La high point.

As with the Nepalese side of the border, trekking in Sikkim is concentrated within two main seasons. For the clearest views and most settled weather, go in the post-monsoon period (October-November), but if you want to enjoy the lush vegetation and abundant wildlife, choose the spring (April-May). The best map to use is *Sikkim Himalaya* at a scale of 1:150,000 published in Bern by the Swiss Foundation for Alpine Research.

*   *   *

THE SINGALILA RIDGE

The highlight of any trek along the ridge will of course be the tremendous Himalayan panorama, closely followed in springtime by the extravagant blossom displays of rhododendron and magnolia. The ridge is well defined and with a number of teahouses and villages spaced along it, and for much of the way trails remain above 3000 metres (9843ft). Although there will inevitably be some steep uphill sections, the paths are never too demanding. In length Singalila treks are in the region of five to seven days, but stages are usually quite short with overnight accommodation that can be arranged either in specially built huts (tourist bungalows and rest houses), or tents.

For a short, five- to six-day trek along what many consider to be the best of the Singalila Ridge, the saddle of Manaybhanjan (2135m: 7005ft), located about 25 kilometres by road from Darjeeling, provides a good place from which to begin, followed by a fairly steep switchback climb to Tonglu on the ridge crest. Two days later the first in a series of magnificent vistas is unveiled, especially from Sandakphu where there is a lodge set at about 3600 metres (11,811ft), from which early morning and evening views of Makalu and the Khumbu giants, plus Kangchenjunga, rival those enjoyed from Chauki on the trek to Kangchenjunga's north side.

Between Sandakphu and Phalut the route traces what is probably the most spectacular section of the ridge with views of a broad sweep of Himalayan snowpeaks being constantly rearranged as you progress towards them. From Phalut a descent through rhododendron forests takes the trek away from the ridge before returning by road to Darjeeling.

It would be possible to trek back to Manaybhanjan from Phalut in just two days, if preferred.

* * *

THE GOECHA LA

The 4940 metre (16,207ft) Goecha La may be a tougher option than the basic Singalila Ridge route, but it is no more spectacular in terms of scenic grandeur. Views of Kangchenjunga are perhaps more dramatic, though, for the mountain's east wall rises just 5 kilometres from the flag-bedecked pass. A seven- to nine-day loop trek from the roadhead at Yuksom usually follows a stay in the Sikkim capital of Gangtok where visits to interesting Buddhist gompas can be arranged.

Yuksom is where the first king of Sikkim was created by three lamas in 1642 at the country's oldest *gompa*. From there the first day's trek makes a long climb through dense, semi-tropical forest of rhododendron, azalea, pine and giant oak trees wrapped in moss, that clothes the Rathong Valley, and ends at Tsoka, the last permanently inhabited village on this route. At the end of the second day - another climb through rhododendrons - the trek reaches the yak pasture of Dzongri (3990m: 13,090ft), with its group of lodges and chortens. By virtue of the altitude at Dzongri, it is advisable to spend a second night here to aid acclimatisation. Some good local walks are available. The area is considered sacred by local Buddhists, and there are fine viewpoints nearby, marked with prayer flags, from which Kangchenjunga, Kabru Dome, Ratong and Koktang are visible. "To watch a sunset from Jongri," wrote D.W.

Freshfield in 1899, "is a thing worth living for." He also predicted that it was destined to become what he called "the Riffel Alp of Sikhim."

Leaving Dzongri the trail follows the moorland-like ridge for a while before descending through forest into the valley of the Prek Chu, across which you climb again to camp at Thangsing in view of glacial moraines and the soaring granite cliffs of nearby Pandim, whose north-west ridge falls steeply to the Goecha La. Next morning the route continues gently up to the turquoise Samite Lake at about 4200 metres (13,779ft). The lake shore is adorned with prayer flags and again there is a choice of camping or of spending the night in a simple trekker's lodge.

The Goecha La is gained directly from Samite Lake. It's a long, toughish climb which leads at first up moraine ridges overlooking the Oglathang Glacier, and is usually tackled by headtorch in order to capture the magic of dawn breaking over the mountains. The La is an impressive place, from which "the stupendous eastern ridge of Kangchenjunga" (Freshfield again) is seen ahead across the Talung Glacier, but clouds often obscure all views by midday, and it is advisable to return to Samite Lake or Thangsing before the build-up begins. It's possible to continue from there to Yuksom by trails other than those taken on the outward trek, and two days should be allowed for this from Samite Lake.

* * *

APPENDIXES

A: CLIMBING KANGCHENJUNGA

The story of Kangchenjunga is a long and interesting one, which proves to be more protracted even than that of the winning of Mount Everest. For a start, the sight of Kangchenjunga from Darjeeling was familiar to many Europeans long before Everest was even recognised for its superior height, and the first Westerner to approach the mountain did so decades before any initial approach was made to the northern slopes of the world's highest mountain. And at a time when both Nepal and Tibet were forbidden lands, because of British influence in Sikkim, Crowley's notorious 1905 expedition predated any attempt to climb Mount Everest by almost twenty years. Kangchenjunga was not climbed until 1955 - two years after Everest was won.

Early Approaches:

1848   The great British botanist Joseph Dalton Hooker made the first of two journeys of exploration that led to within a few kilometres of Kangchenjunga. The first took him across the Singalila Ridge into Nepal, from where he trekked a circuitous route to the head of the Tamur River, then over the mountains to Ghunsa (which he mistakenly called Khambachen) and on to the south side of Kangchenjunga. The following year he travelled up the Teesta Valley in Sikkim, and attempted Lamgebo Peak. After this he tried to reach the Zemu Glacier, explored the Lachen and Lachung valleys and made attempts on Kangchenjau and Pauhunri. Hooker also made a small-scale map of Sikkim.

1852   Captain W.S. Sherwill, a British Revenue Surveyor, studied the geology of the Kangchenjunga massif, and also conducted a partial survey of the region and mapped the headwaters of the Ringbi, Yunga and Yalung rivers.

1855   Hermann von Schlagintweit, a German working on the Magnetic Survey of India, journeyed north along the Singalila Ridge and painted panoramic views of both Everest and Kangchenjunga before being turned back by Nepalese soldiers.

1861   Major J.L. Sherwill trekked with three companions to the Goecha La and gazed on Kangchenjunga's east wall across the Talung Glacier.

1876   Crossing into Nepal by the Kang La, Mrs Elizabeth Sarah Mazuchelli approached the south side of Jannu - a journey recorded in *The Indian Alps and How We Crossed Them*.

1879   The pundit Babu Sarat Chandra Das, made a journey into Tibet with the lama Ugyen Gyatsho, passing close to the base of Kangchenjunga. Two years later he was back again, crossing the Nango La north of Khambachen. In 1883 Lama Ugyen Gyatsho travelled to Lhasa by way of the

Dongkya La. A map was produced which shows country to the north of the Kangchenjunga massif.

1883 Work started in 1878 by Captain H.J. Harman to survey the Sikkim Himalaya, was completed in 1883 by W. Robert when he explored rivers flowing from Kangchenjunga's eastern and south-western flanks.

This same year W.W. Graham and his Swiss guides climbed several peaks of around 6000 metres in the Kangchenjunga massif. His claim to have made the first ascent of Kabru was disputed·at the time, although he had some influential supporters. If he did climb Kabru it was the highest summit reached for many years.

1884 Pundit Rinsing (Rinzin Namgyal), who had aided W. Robert's survey by exploring the Talung Valley, was the first to approach the south-west face of Kangchenjunga when he reached 5800 metres from the Yalung Glacier. He went on to follow the route taken by Chandra Das across the Mirgin and Sinion Las, and continued back to Darjeeling. In so doing he achieved the first complete circuit of Kangchenjunga.

1891 During his time as Political Officer in Sikkim, J.C. White travelled extensively in that country. In 1890 he crossed the Goecha La, and in 1891 went up the Zemu Glacier with the photographer T. Hoffmann. White went on through the Lhonak Valley as far as the Naku La on the Tibetan border.

1899 D.W. Freshfield, together with the pundit Rinsing, Edmund Garwood, C. Dover, Vittorio and Erminio Sella, a photographic assistant named Botta, and the Val Tournanche guide Angelo Maquinaz, made a seven-week circuit of the Kangchenjunga massif, described in *Round Kangchenjunga*.

Expeditions:

1905 The first attempt to climb Kangchenjunga was made by a group of three Swiss (Dr J. Jacot-Guillarmod, Lieutenant Alexis Pache and C.A. Reymond) under the leadership of Aleister Crowley, who invited along an Italian hotelier from Darjeeling, Riga de Righi. The party crossed into Nepal and ascended the Yalung Glacier, placing their Camp 7 at about 6200 metres (20,341ft). From there a high point about 300 metres above the camp was reached. On September 1, Guillarmod, Pache, de Righi and three porters were descending to a lower camp when two of the porters fell, setting off a small avalanche. Lieutenant Pache and the porters were buried beneath three metres of snow, while de Righi was half-buried. He and Guillarmod had to cut the rope to free themselves. Hearing cries for help, Reymond alone descended to offer assistance, while Crowley, by his own admission, remained in the upper camp drinking tea. "Not that I was over anxious in the circumstances to render help," he wrote. "A mountain 'accident' of this sort is one of the things for which I have no sympathy whatever...the doctor is old enough to rescue himself, and nobody would want to rescue Righi." Seemingly unmoved by the four deaths, in another report to the *Daily Mail*, dated September 9, Crowley said: "As the avalanche was neither large nor steep, I am of the opinion that if a rope had not been employed the accident would not have happened. In consequence of this loss of life, I declined to assume further responsibility and returned with the remainder of the expedition. I am not altogether disappointed with the present results. I know enough to make certain of success another year with a properly equipped and disciplined expedition."

1907   The retiring Scottish scientist Dr A.M. Kellas visited the Zemu Glacier and made two attempts to reach the Nepal Gap. In subsequent years he made a whole series of climbs and explorations around the Kangchenjunga region, always with native companions, and at the time of the first expedition to Mount Everest in 1921 (during which he died of a heart attack on the approach march) was one of the most experienced of all Himalayan mountaineers.

1920   Harold Raeburn and C.G. Crawford made a reconnaissance of the Yalung side of the mountain. Rather than follow the line of Crowley's 1905 route, they tended more to the east, towards the Talung Saddle, but were discouraged by serious avalanche danger. "The roar of the ice avalanches from Kangchen and Talung seldom ceased for long, day and night." After retreating, they made what may well have been the first crossing of the Ratong La, although Raeburn speculated that it could possibly have been used by early migrations of Tibetans into Sikkim.

1929   A young and inexperienced American, E.F. Farmer, set out with the secret intention of climbing Kangchenjunga alone. On May 26 he left Camp 3 with Lobsang (who was to serve as Sirdar on the 1930 International Expedition) and two ex-Everest porters, and during the morning told his companions to wait for him as he planned to climb higher in order to take photographs. Farmer failed to return that night, but next day was seen climbing towards the Talung Saddle. Clouds then intervened and he was never seen again.

During the summer monsoon a powerful German expedition under the leadership of Paul Bauer marched to the Zemu Glacier with a plan to attempt Kangchenjunga's Eastern Spur, the crest of which was gained on September 16. From that point a precarious route was created up, around and through towers and mushrooms of ice and snow. Camps 8, 9 and 10 were dug into ice caves, the highest being at about 7100 metres (23,294ft). On October 3, Allwein and Kraus left Camp 10 and ploughed through deep snow to a high point of about 7400 metres (24,278ft) when a blizzard began which lasted five days. Retreat was made extremely difficult and hazardous, but the whole team evacuated the mountain without loss, but in poor condition. This attempt was described at the time as "a feat without parallel, perhaps, in all the annals of mountaineering." Comparing the respective difficulties of Kangchenjunga and Everest, E.F. Norton wrote: "Events may well prove me wrong: but on the face of it, Kangchenjunga appears to me a more dangerous proposition than Mount Everest." History has not proved him wrong.

162

1930 Under the leadership of Professor G.O. Dyhrenfurth, an International Expedition comprising five Germans, three British, two Swiss and an Austrian chose to attack the North Ridge via the Northwest Face, permission for which was received from the Maharajah of Nepal as the expedition was about to leave Darjeeling in early April. The expedition crossed into Nepal via the Kang La, then took the route over the Mirgin La and Sinion La to Ghunsa, Khambachen and Pangpema. In early May two camps were pitched between Pangpema and a series of ice cliffs. On May 9, the way to Camp 3 was being opened when a huge section of ice wall broke off and overwhelmed Sherpa Chettan. The attempt by this route was immediately abandoned, and attention turned to the Northwest Ridge. Wieland and Schneider reached the top of a big rock tower at about 6400 metres (21,000ft) before turning back. "The difficulties of the north-west ridge are amazing," wrote Dyhrenfurth later, "as great as or greater than those of the north-east spur. That alone would not have discouraged us, for technical difficulties are generally a question of time. But time here was our greatest enemy."

1931 Bauer returned with a second German expedition consisting of 11 climbers, to continue where he had left off in 1929. Advanced Base (Camp 6) was established on July 13, but if anything, conditions were even worse on the mountain than they had been on his previous attempt, and it took two months of hard work to make the most difficult section of the route passable. Sirdar Lobsang and a porter fell ill and died, and while on the way to Camp 8 Hermann Schaller and Pasang were killed by a fall from a ridge tower. Camp 11, dug into an ice cave at 7360 metres (24,147ft), was not placed until September 15, and on gaining the Eastern Spur above it, conditions were thought to be too dangerous to continue. Bauer's second attempt to climb Kangchenjunga had thereby failed, this time with the loss of four lives.

1936 Bauer again returned to the Kangchenjunga massif, this time making an attempt on the East Summit of the Twins (Gimmigela) by way of the East Ridge. Once more he was thwarted by heavy monsoon snow.

1937 A three-man expedition consisting of the Swiss, Ernst Grob, and two Germans (Ludwig Schmaderer and Herbert Paider) visited the Zemu Basin and made another unsuccessful attempt on the Twins. Had they been successful, it was thought this route might offer a way onto Kangchenjunga's North Ridge via the North Col. (These three went on to make the second ascent of Siniolchu in Sikkim.)

In the autumn a small British party (C.R. Cooke, with John and Joy Hunt) prospected the eastern side of Kangchenjunga, during which Cooke, with Dawa Thondup, Pasang Kikuli and Kitar attempted to reach the North Col. Cooke reached a point about 100 metres below the Col before a bombardment of wind-propelled stones and lumps of ice forced a retreat.

1939 Grob, Schmaderer and Paider climbed Tent Peak and made the third ascent of Nepal Peak, but heavy monsoon snow once again defeated their attempt to climb the Twins.

1953   Following distant study of the Southwest Face of Kangchenjunga with the Swiss, Georg Frey, in 1951, Gilmour Lewis returned to the Yalung Glacier region with John Kempe and 36 porters to attempt neighbouring peaks from which they could make a more detailed survey of the face. Unobstructed views revealed a feasible route above the Great Shelf, although the lower face appeared to be very difficult and in need of close scrutiny.

1954   Everest having been climbed in 1953, and K2 in '54, Kangchenjunga now assumed a new importance as the world's highest unclimbed mountain. With this in mind, Kempe and Lewis returned to the Yalung Glacier region in the spring with four other climbers, charged with the objective of either setting foot on one of the main ridges leading to the summit, or to reach the great ice shelf which runs across the Southwest Face and which is visible from Darjeeling. After investigating three possible routes, the party reported back to a special Sub-Committee of the Alpine Club, formed under Sir John Hunt's chairmanship, to prepare for a full-scale Kangchenjunga expedition.

1955   With a sense of urgency in regard to Kangchenjunga, a strong British party led by Charles Evans (who, with Tom Bourdillon, had reached the South Summit of Everest in 1953) left Darjeeling in March. The expedition crossed the Singalila and trekked to Ramze beside the Yalung Glacier, which they reached on the 24th. Loads were then ferried along the glacier to Base Camp at the foot of the Lower Icefall. After attempting Kempe's Buttress, which proved too dangerous, New Zealander Norman Hardie and George Band forced a way through the icefall ("it made the Everest icefall seem like a children's playground" said Band who had also been on the successful '53 expedition) to Camp 2, pitched at about 6200 metres (20,400ft). The Upper Icefall proved to be much easier than expected, and Camp 3 was sited against a solid wall of ice on a platform at 6645 metres (21,800ft). Using bottled oxygen Evans, Hardie and two Sherpas set off on May 12 and reached the lower edge of the Great Shelf where they pitched Camp 4 (7163m: 23,500ft). The Sherpas were then sent down and next day Evans and Hardie found a route over crevasse-free slopes to a spacious ledge chosen as the site for Camp 5 (7710m: 25,300ft). Loads were carried up and cached there on the 19th, but that night a blizzard set in that lasted 60 hours. When May 22 dawned clear it was found that an avalanche had hit the site of the unmanned Camp 5, scattering or burying food and equipment. As much as possible of this had to be found, dug out and hauled back up before work could begin on the route to Camp 6. This was placed near the top of the Gangway on the 24th, and from there, on May 25 in perfect weather, Band and Joe Brown set out for the summit at 8.15am. Emerging onto the West Ridge nearly 4 hours later they stopped for a quick snack, then continued, at first on easier ground, then coming to an abrupt tower of brown and grey rock, whose right-hand side was broken by several vertical cracks. Rock specialist Joe Brown led up one of these - the hardest part of the whole climb, according to Band. At the top of this rose a gently sloping cone of snow that led to the summit. It was 2.45pm. In accordance with the wishes of the Sikkimese, to whom Kangchenjunga is a sacred mountain, the actual summit was left untrodden, and next day when Norman Hardie and Tony Streather also got to within a few paces of the top, they too left it unsullied.

Highlights Since 1955

For nearly twenty years after the first ascent, the Kangchenjunga massif was practically ignored by mountaineers. Political difficulties in gaining permission to climb either in Sikkim or in eastern Nepal were partly responsible for this, but so too was the sheer number of other 'big' mountains that remained virgin at this time. It has also been suggested that Kangchenjunga's status as a holy mountain also acted as a deterrent. But Kangchenjunga consists of several summits, all except the highest of which were still as yet unclimbed, so when climbers did return their attention to the massif, it was to claim the secondary summits, as well as to attempt new routes to the main peak.

1965 Kangbachen was attempted by a 12-man team from Yugoslavia via the Ramtang Glacier. A high point on the ridge between the main summit and Pt.7532m was gained late in the afternoon of October 13 by Sasonov, Dimitrov and two Sherpas. Despite having neither tents nor proper bivouac equipment, the Yugoslavs decided to spend the night out at 7453 metres (24,475ft) while the Sherpas descended to Camp 5. The following morning Sasonov and Dimitrov were forced to abandon their attempt through severe frostbite.

1973 In the pre-monsoon season, Yalung Kang (formerly Kang-chenjunga's West Peak) was climbed from the south by Takeo Matsuda and Yutaka Ageta from the Kyoto University Academic Alpine Club of Japan. The pair reached the summit late on May 14 and bivouaced on the way down at about 8220 metres (26,970ft). Sadly, Matsuda fell to his death on the descent.

1974 A 15-man Polish expedition made the first ascent of Kangbachen via the Northwest Face.

1977 Twenty-two years after the first ascent, Kangchenjunga's main peak received its second ascent, this time by Major Prem Chand and Naik Nima Dorje Sherpa of a large Indian Army expedition. Rather than repeat the 1955 route, this expedition attacked the Eastern Spur which had twice defeated Bauer.

1978 Kangchenjunga's South Summit was won by a Polish expedition which gained the Great Shelf using the route of the 1955 British expedition from the Yalung Glacier, then took a broad gully leading from the Shelf up to the South Buttress. Chrobak and Wróz reached the South Summit on May 18. At the same time a Spanish team with a permit to attempt Yalung Kang, joined forces with the Polish expedition and climbed the three 'humps' which constitute Kangchenjunga's Central Summit. Leaders of both expeditions were subsequently punished for having "climbed peaks other than those for which they were granted permission".

1979 The third ascent of Kangchenjunga was achieved in fine, oxygen-free style by Doug Scott, Peter Boardman and Joe Tasker of a four-man expedition via the North Col, the first expedition to attempt the mountain from the northwest since the International Expedition of 1930. (Frenchman Georges Bettembourg missed out on the actual summit climb.)

1980   When climbing the North Col route in 1979 Scott's party avoided the ice terraces and sérac barriers of the Northwest Face, by tackling the steep rock and ice at its left-hand end. In 1980 a Japanese expedition forced a direct route up the face and reached the summit on May 17. However, unlike the British in 1955 and '79, and the Indians in '77, the Japanese ignored the sacred nature of the summit and (in Doug Scott's words) "trod all over the top!" Until now Kangchenjunga had been the untrodden peak.

1983   The first true solo ascent of Kangchenjunga was achieved in the post-monsoon season by Pierre Béghin who climbed the Southwest Face (1955 route) from Base Camp to summit in just three days.

1984   A large Japanese expedition set up a series of camps at the head of the Yalung Glacier with the aim of making the first traverse of Kang-chenjunga's summit ridge. Between May 18 and 20, Seishi Wada and Toichiro Mitani climbed the South, Central and Main summits. Their route took them along the ridge between the South and Central summits, then they descended to the Great Shelf and joined the 1955 route to the Main Summit. Yalung Kang (the West Summit) was not climbed on this occasion.

1989   The full traverse of the four main peaks of Kangchenjunga was won by a 30-member Soviet team led by Eduard Myslovski, supported by 17 Sherpas. Not only did they make the traverse in both directions, but also added new routes to the Main Summit and the difficult South Summit. Setting out from a high camp on April 30, a five-member team under the leadership of Sergei Bershov, climbed Yalung Kang and continued over the next two summits to reach the South Summit at 2.45pm on May 1. The second team, heading westward, was met on the saddle between the South and Central summits. In all, members of this Soviet expedition made a total of 85 individual ascents.

Given the geography of the massif, this traverse was, perhaps, an inevitable development of sporting activity on the world's third highest mountain. But it came at a time when climbing focus in the Himalaya was turning away from large-scale expeditions, with major innovations now coming from lightweight teams attempting alpine-style ascents. In this, Kangchenjunga has no shortage of challenges for mountaineers at the sharp end of the sport, for despite the massive nature of its huge walls, individual summits and long ridges, the mountain has no easy routes. Every face is ravaged by objective dangers, its ridges are both long and difficult. No less important is the fact that it attracts the full force of the monsoon, and receives greater precipitation than any other 8000 metre peak.

So, despite the many decades of attention and activity, Kangchenjunga remains the mountaineer's mountain.

* * *

APPENDIX B: USEFUL ADDRESSES

1: Selected Overseas Missions of the Nepalese Government:

Embassies:

UK
12a Kensington Palace Gardens
London W8 4QU
(Tel: 0171 229 1594)

France
7 rue de Washington
75008 Paris
(Tel: 435 92861)

USA
2131 Leroy Place
Washington
DC 20008 (Tel: 202 667 4550)

Germany
Im-Hag 15
Bad Godesberg 2
D-5300 Bonn (Tel: 0228 343097)

Consulates:

USA
820 Second Avenue, Suite 202
New York
NY 10017 (Tel: 212 370 4188)

473 Jackson Street
San Francisco
CA 94111
(Tel: 415 434 1111)

Canada
310 Dupont Street
Toronto, Ontario
(Tel: 416 968 7252)

Australia
870 Military Road, Suite 1,
Strand Centre, Mosman, Sydney
NSW 2088 (Tel: 960 3565)

2: Selected Foreign Missions in Nepal:

British Embassy
Lainchaur, Kathmandu
(Tel: 411789/410583)

Australian Embassy
Bhat Bhatani, Kathmandu
(Tel: 411578)

American Embassy
Pani Pokhari
Kathmandu
(Tel: 411179/411601)

The following countries also have Embassies located in or near Kathmandu:

China: Baluwatar
France: Lazimpat
Germany: Kantipath
India: Lainchaur
Israel: Lazimpat
Italy: Baluwatar

Japan: Pani Pokhari
Korea (North): Patan
Korea (South): Tahachal
Pakistan: Pani Pokhari
Thailand: Thapathali

The following countries have Kathmandu-based Consulates:

Austria: Kupondole
Belgium: Lazimpat
Denmark: Kantipath
Finland: Khichpokhari

Netherlands: Kumaripati
Sweden: Khichpokhari
Switzerland: Jawalakhel

In addition, the following Cultural Centres are based in Kathmandu:

The British Council
Kantipath (Tel: 211305)

United States Information Service
New Road (Tel: 211250)

French Cultural Centre
Bag Bazar (Tel: 214326)

3: Useful Addresses for Trekking in Sikkim (India):

Office of the High Commissioner for
India
India House, Aldwych
London WC2 4NA
(Tel: 0171 437 3677/8)

British High Commission
Chanakyapuri, New Delhi 110-021
India
(Tel: 690371)

Selected Government of India Tourist Offices:

U.K.
7 Cork Street
London W1X 2AB
(Tel: 0171 437 3677)

Australia
Level 5, 65 Elizabeth Street
Sydney, NSW 2000
(Tel: (02) 232 1600)

USA
30 Rockefeller Plaza, Suite 15
North Mezzanine
New York, NY 10020
(Tel: 212 586 4901)

Canada
60 Bloor Street, West Suite No 1003
Toronto
Ontario M4 W3 B8
(Tel: 416 962 3787)

4: Map Suppliers:

Cordee
3a De Montfort Street
Leicester LE1 7HD
(Tel: 0116 2543579)

Edward Stanford Ltd
12-14 Long Acre
London WC2E 9LP
(Tel: 0171 240 3611)

Bradt Enterprises Inc
95 Harvey Street
Cambridge
MA 02140 USA

Michael Chessler Books
PO Box 2436
Evergreen
CO 80439 USA

Note: There are many booksellers in Kathmandu who stock trekking maps for the Kangchenjunga region. Try Pilgrims in Thamel (near the Kathmandu Guesthouse).

5: Health Advice for Travellers:

MASTA (Medical Advisory Service
for Travellers Abroad)
Keppel Street
London WC1E 7HT

(Telephone Travellers' Help Line:
01891 224 100)

6: Insurance for Trekkers (UK):

Bishopgate Insurance Ltd
Bishopgate House
Tollgate, Eastleigh
Hants SO53 3YA
(Tel: 01703 644455)

British Mountaineering Council
(for BMC members only)
177-179 Burton Road
Manchester M20 2BB
(Tel: 0161 445 4747)

Campbells Irvine Ltd
48 Earls Court Road, Kensington
London W8 6EJ
(Tel: 0171 937 6981)

P.J. Hayman & Co Ltd
Forestry House
New Barn Road
Buriton, nr Petersfield
Hants GU31 5SL
(Tel: 01730 260222)

Snowcard
FREEPOST 4135
Lower Boddington
Daventry
Northants NN11 6BR
(Tel: 01327 263227)

* * *

APPENDIX C: TREKKING AGENCIES

The following list is not a comprehensive one, but is offered as a guide only. Many other agents, both in the UK and in Kathmandu, offer treks in the Kangchenjunga region, but it should be borne in mind that as businesses come and go, and occasionally change their names, some of those actually listed might not survive this edition. *Please note that mention of any trekking agent in this book should not necessarily be seen as an endorsement of that company's service.*

1: Nepal-based Agents:

Note: to telephone Nepal from the UK dial 00 (International code), then 977 + 1 (for Kathmandu) followed by the individual number.

Ang Rita Trek & Expedition
PO Box 7232
Thamel, Kathmandu
(Tel: 226577 Fax: 977 1 229459)

Highland Sherpa Trekking
PO Box 3597
Jyatha Tole, Kathmandu
(Tel: 226487)

Himalayan Explorers
PO Box 1737
Thamel, Kathmandu
(Tel: 226142)

Himalayan Paradise Trekking
PO Box 5343
Chabahil, Kathmandu
(Tel: 475744 Fax: 977 1 471103)

2: Trekking Agents Based in the United Kingdom:

Bufo Ventures
3 Elim Grove, Windermere LA23 2JN
(Tel: 015394 45445)

Classic Nepal
33 Metro Avenue, Newton,
Derbyshire DE55 5UF
(Tel: 01773 873497)

Exodus
9 Weir Road
London SW12 0LT
(Tel: 0181 675 5550)

KE Adventure Travel
32 Lake Road, Keswick
Cumbria CA12 5DQ
(Tel: 017687 73966)

Explorasia
Sloan Square House, Holbein Place
London SW1W 8NS
(Tel: 0171 973 0482)

Nepal Trekking
10 Swinbourne Street
Hull HU8 8LY
(Tel: 01482 703135)

Explore Worldwide
1 Frederick Street, Aldershot
Hants GU11 1LQ
(Tel: 01252 344161)

Ramblers Holidays
Box 43, Welwyn Garden City
Herts AL8 6PQ
(Tel: 01707 331133)

Guerba Expeditions
101 Eden Vale Road, Westbury
Wilts BA13 3QX
(Tel: 01373 826611)

Sherpa Expeditions
131a Heston Road, Hounslow
Middlesex TW5 0RD
(Tel: 0181 577 7187)

High Places
Globe Works, Penistone Road
Sheffield S6 3AE
(Tel: 0114 2757500)

Specialist Trekking Cooperative
Chapel House, Low Cotehill
Nr Carlisle, Cumbria CA4 0EL
(Tel: 01228 562368)

Himalayan Kingdoms
20 The Mall, Clifton
Bristol BS8 4DR
Tel: (0117 9237163)

Worldwide Journeys & Expeditions
8 Comeragh Road
London W14 9HP
(Tel: 0171 381 8638)

* * *

APPENDIX D: GLOSSARY

An ability to speak a few words of Nepali will greatly enhance the experience of trekking in Nepal, for whilst your Sirdar, and probably a few other members of the crew, will have some command of English (and quite possibly several other languages too), it is both useful and polite to be able to communicate with villagers along the way in their own language. As trekking and mountaineering expeditions become more numerous throughout Eastern Nepal, so English will become more widely understood. Yet an attempt to speak a few words of the host tongue will reap dividends.

The following glossary lists a selection of words that may be found useful on trek. However, there are several Nepali phrasebooks and dictionaries available in Kathmandu bookshops (and also found increasingly in the West) that would be worth consulting. In addition, Dr Stephen Bezruchka's highly recommended language tape and accompanying book

Nepali for Trekkers (The Mountaineers, 1991) provides an essential guide to pronunciation and grammar. Lonely Planet publish a small, lightweight *Nepal Phrasebook* that would fit easily into a shirt pocket for instant use along the trail.

aaja	-	today	dhara	-	waterspout
aalu	-	potatoes	dharmsala	-	pilgrims' resthouse
ama	-	mother	dherai	-	many, much
ava	-	father	dokan	-	shop (see pasal)
baato	-	trail	doko	-	conical load-carrying basket used by porters
baayaan	-	left (direction)			
banthanti	-	the place in the forest			
			drangka	-	stream (see also nadi)
bazaar	-	market	dudh	-	milk
bhanjyang	-	foothill pass	gaau	-	village (see also gaon)
bhat	-	cooked rice	gaon	-	village (see also gaau)
bhatti	-	traditional inn or guest-house	ghar	-	house (see also khangba)
bholi	-	tomorrow	gompa	-	Buddhist temple or monastery
Bhot	-	Tibet			
Bhotiya	-	Buddhist people of mountain Nepal	goth	-	herdsman's shelter
			hijo	-	yesterday
bistaari	-	slowly	himal	-	snow mountain
chang	-	home-made beer	ho	-	yes
chapaati	-	unleavened bread (see also roti)	hoina	-	no
			kang	-	mountain
charpi	-	toilet	kani	-	covered archway, or entrance chorten, decorated with Buddhist motifs
chaulki	-	police post			
chautaara	-	trailside resting place			
			kata	-	Buddhist ceremonial scarf
chini	-	sugar			
chiso paani	-	cold water	khaana	-	food
chiyaa	-	tea	khangba	-	house (see also ghar)
chorpen	-	temple guardian	kharka	-	high pasture
chorten	-	Buddhist shrine, like an elaborate cairn	khola	-	river (see also kosi)
			kosi	-	river (see also khola)
daahine	-	right (direction)	kot	-	fortress
daal bhat	-	staple meal of Nepal; rice with lentil sauce	kripaya	-	please
			kukri	-	Ghurka knife with curved blade (sometimes spelt khukari)
danda	-	ridge (in foothills)			
deorali	-	pass on a ridge	kund	-	lake (see also pokhari, tal and tsho)
dhai	-	yoghurt			
dhanyabaad	-	thank you	la	-	high pass (Tibetan)

lama	-	Buddhist monk or priest
lekh	-	hill, or foothill ridge
lho	-	south
maasu	-	meat
maati baato-		upper trail
mandir	-	Hindu temple
mani	-	Buddhist prayer, from the mantra 'Om Mani Padme Hum'
mani wall	-	stone wall carved with Buddhist mantras
mantra	-	religious incantation
momo	-	stuffed savoury pastry, or dumpling
naalaa	-	small stream
nadi	-	stream (Hindi: see also drangka)
namaskar	-	more polite form of namaste
namaste	-	traditional greeting; it means 'I salute the god within you'
namlo	-	porter's headband
nun	-	salt
nup	-	west
paani	-	water (see also chiso paani, taato paani and umaleko paani)
panchayat	-	system of local government/area council
pasal	-	shop (see also dokan)
phedi	-	literally, 'the place at the foot of the hill'
phul	-	egg
pokhari	-	lake (see also kund, tal and tsho)
puja	-	religious offering, or prayer
pul	-	bridge (see also sangu)
raamro	-	good
raamro chaaina	-	not good

raati	-	night
rakshi	-	distilled spirit, made from grain
ri	-	mountain peak
Rimpoche	-	reincarnated priest
roti	-	bread (see also chapaati)
saano	-	small
sadhu	-	Hindu ascetic
sangu	-	bridge (see also pul)
satu	-	flour
shaligram	-	ammonite
shar	-	east
Sherpa	-	ethnic people of Solu-Khumbu
Sherpani	-	female Sherpa (also denotes a female porter)
sida	-	straight ahead (direction)
sirdar	-	man in charge of a trek crew
stupa	-	large chorten
suntala	-	orange (fruit)
taato paani-		hot water
tal	-	lake (see also kund, pokhari and tsho)
thanka	-	Buddhist scroll painting
thanti	-	place
thukpa	-	noodle soup
thulo	-	big
trisul	-	trident symbol of followers of Shiva
tsampa	-	roasted barley flour
tsho	-	lake (see also kund, pokhari and tal)
ukaalo	-	steep uphill
umaleko paani	-	boiled water
yersa	-	collection of herdsmen's shelters or summer settlement

Days of the Week:			16	-	sohra
Aitobaar	-	Sunday	17	-	satra
Sombaar	-	Monday	18	-	athaara
Mangalbaar	-	Tuesday	19	-	unnaais
Budhbaar	-	Wednesday	20	-	bis
Bihibaar	-	Thursday	25	-	pachhis
Sukrobaar	-	Friday	30	-	tis
Sanibaar	-	Saturday	35.	-	paitis
			40	-	chaalis
Numbers:			45	-	paitaalis
1	-	ek	50	-	pachaas
2	-	dui	55	-	pachpanna
3	-	tin	60	-	saathi
4	-	char	65	-	paisatthi
5	-	paanch	70	-	sattari
6	-	chha	75	-	pachahattar
7	-	saat	80	-	ashi
8	-	aath	85	-	pachaasi
9	-	nau	90	-	nabbe
10	-	das	95	-	panchaanaabbe
11	-	eghaara	100	-	ek sae
12	-	baahra	1000	-	ek hajaar
13	-	tehra	1/2	-	aadha
14	-	chaudha	1 1/2	-	dedh
15	-	pandhra			

* * *

BIBLIOGRAPHY

There are numerous English-language books about Nepal and/or the Himalaya that will add interest to anyone planning a visit to the Kangchenjunga region. The following list provides a fairly wide sample. Inevitably some titles are out of print and unobtainable in the West, other than by special order through public libraries. But many bookshops in Kathmandu stock an admirable selection of new, old and reprinted volumes, and will be worth investigating if you cannot find what you want at home.

1: General Tourist Guides:
The number of general guides to Nepal grows almost yearly. Perhaps the best and most comprehensive of those available at present are:
Insight Guide: Nepal edited by Hans Höfer (APA Publications). Expert contributions, both textual and photographic, give this regularly-updated book an air of authority.
The Insider's Guide to Nepal by Brian Tetley (Moorland Publishing, 1991) with

many fine photographs by Mohamed Amin and Duncan Willetts. Among more general information, it briefly describes a 16-day trek to Kangchenjunga, written before the road went as far as Basantpur.

Nepal (Nelles Guides published by Nelles Verlag / Robertson McCarta, 1990) includes a small section on the trek to Kangchenjunga.

Nepal: The Rough Guide by David Reed (Rough Guides / Penguin Books, 1993) and *Nepal: A Travel Survival Kit* by Tony Wheeler and Richard Everist (Lonely Planet, 1993) both offer lots of practical no-nonsense advice on getting around Nepal, and include some trekking information.

Not a tourist guide as such, the following large-format book is packed with an assortment of information and photographs gleaned from the author's wide-ranging travels. *Nepal: The Kingdom of the Himalayas* by Toni Hagen (Kümmerly and Frey, 1980) is the definitive work on the people and geography of the country, and is highly recommended. Employed in the 1950s as a government geologist, Hagen, an engineer and natural scientist, was the first man to be given the freedom to explore the whole of Nepal, and as such his knowledge, gleaned over a period of eight years, must be considered unique.

2: Photographic Books:

Nepal's rich visual splendour counts as one of the major trekking attractions. The two landscape-format books mentioned below provide obvious temptations in the superb photographic images reproduced. Only the first includes illustrations taken in the Kangchenjunga area, while the second is very much a souvenir of the trekking experience. Both are recommended.

Heart of the Himalaya by David Paterson (Peak Publishing, 1997)

People Within A Landscape by Bert Willison & Shirley Bourke (The Mountaineers, Seattle, USA / The Four Sherpa Trust, New Plymouth, NZ, 1989)

3: Trekking:

Most trekking guides to Nepal attempt to cover as many areas as possible. Each one contains plenty of interest and practical advice, but for the majority of trekkers whose visit concentrates on just one route or one region only, there will inevitably be large passages of unused material.

Trekking in Nepal by Stephen Bezruchka (Cordee / The Mountaineers - 7th edition, 1997) is *the* classic trekker's guide. Packed with information, it is a gem of a book. Sensitively written and regularly updated, the author's commitment to the country and his concern for the people are examples to all who follow in his footsteps. Anyone planning to visit Nepal should study this book before leaving home.

Trekking in the Nepal Himalaya by Stan Armington (Lonely Planet - 7th edition, 1997) is another weighty guide to several trekking regions, including Kangchenjunga. The author has spent many years leading trekking parties in the Himalaya, and lives in Kathmandu. The latest edition contains plenty of up-to-the-minute information.

Trekking in Nepal by Toru Nakano (Springfield Books, 1990) has a strong photographic content, but poor text. Some of the illustrations are particularly striking and will be a reminder to take a camera and plenty of film with you.

Trekking in Nepal, West Tibet and Bhutan by Hugh Swift (Sierra Club/Hodder & Stoughton, 1989) provides a stimulating overview of numerous trekking possibilities in these three countries, including a small section about a trek to Kangchenjunga made in the 1980s by Anne Frej. The book covers too much territory to give precise detail, but makes enjoyable reading nonetheless. A much more personal book than the three mentioned above, it is enlivened by anecdotes that really make you want to pull on your boots and go.

Trekking in Pakistan and India by Hugh Swift (Sierra Books/Hodder & Stoughton, 1990) is a companion volume to the above book. It contains a small section devoted to Sikkim.

4: Mountain Exploration & Mountaineering:

This is the largest selection, for it contains a number of titles devoted to mountaineering attempts on Kangchenjunga which will provide background interest.

Himalayan Journals by Joseph Dalton Hooker (John Murray, 1855 - latest revised & condensed edition by Today & Tomorrow's Printers & Publishers, New Delhi, 1987). This is a classic of Himalayan travel literature that includes an account of Hooker's journeys to Kangchenjunga in 1848-49. Should be obtainable in Kathmandu.

Round Kangchenjunga by D.W. Freshfield (Arnold, 1903 - latest edition published by Ratna Pustak Bhandar, Kathmandu, 1979). At times turgid, at times inspired, Freshfield's account of his circuit of Kangchenjunga in 1899 nonetheless makes interesting reading for anyone planning to trek there.

The Kangchenjunga Adventure by F.S. Smythe (Victor Gollancz, 1930) is an account of the 1930 International Expedition to the northwest side of the mountain.

Himalayan Campaign: The German Attack on Kangchenjunga by Paul Bauer (Blackwell, 1937) is the story of Bauer's two attempts in 1929 and '31.

Kangchenjunga Challenge by Paul Bauer (Kimber, 1955) is very much a rewrite of his earlier book.

Kanchenjunga by John Tucker (Elek Books, 1955). The reconnaissance expedition of 1954, which discovered the route taken by Evans' team the following year.

Kangchenjunga, the Untrodden Peak by Charles Evans (Hodder, 1956). The story of the first ascent in 1955, by the leader of the expedition.

Kangchenjunga: First Ascent from the North-East Spur by Col. Narinder Kumar (Vision Books, 1978). As the title suggests, this is the story of the Indian Army ascent of Kangchenjunga in 1977, the second overall, but first via the

Northeast Spur.

Sacred Summits by Peter Boardman (Hodder, 1982) and *Savage Arena* by Joe Tasker (Methuen, 1982). Both volumes contain accounts of the 1979 ascent via the North Col, now brought together as part of *The Boardman Tasker Omnibus* (Bâton Wicks/The Mountaineers, 1996).

Himalayan Climber by Doug Scott (Diadem Books, 1992) is a showcase for Scott's tremendous photography. It includes a section devoted to his 1979 ascent of Kangchenjunga with Boardman, Tasker and Bettembourg.

Living on the Edge: The Winter Ascent of Kangchenjunga by Cherie Bremer-Kamp (David & Charles, 1987). The subtitle is misleading. This is the story of a winter attempt in 1985 by Bremer-Kamp and Chris Chandler, with Nima Tensing (kitchen boy on Scott's expedition), which ended when Chandler died of pulmonary oedema.

At Grips with Jannu by Jean Franco & Lionel Terray (Victor Gollancz, 1967) is the account of the French ascent of Jannu in 1962.

To the Third Pole: the History of the High Himalayas by G.O. Dyhrenfurth (Laurie, 1955). A history of attempts on the 8000m peaks, it includes attempts on Kangchenjunga prior to the first ascent.

Sivalaya: the 8000-metre Peaks of the Himalaya by Louis Baume (Gastons-West Col, 1978). Similar to Dyhrenfurth's book, but in more concise form, and inevitably more up-to-date in content.

High Asia: An Illustrated History of the 7000 metre Peaks by Jill Neate (Unwin Hyman, 1989). Synopses of the ascent of the Himalayan 7000m peaks by a noted bibliophile, with brief accounts of several mountains within the Kangchenjunga region.

* * *